Saving Your Way to Success

Saving Your Way to Success

By

Justin P. Ertelt

ISBN: 1-58820-099-X (Paperback)

This book is printed on acid free paper.

1stBooks - rev. 01/24/03

About this Book

Saving Your Way to Success is not your average how-to-save-money book. This unique financial self-help book incorporates concrete tips on how to save with a twist of inspiration to motivate you to achieve your financial goals.

Why should you save money? How do you start? How can you become successful through saving?

Making saving money a habit to maximize your savings potential is the foundation for financial freedom set forth in *Saving Your Way to Success.* This money-saving book takes the way we think about saving and turns it into an idea that can revolutionize how and why we save. Corroborating research and study, personal experience and time-tested methods of saving, this book is proof that working hard and saving money are the keys to the accumulation of long-term wealth and the achievement of financial success.

Has a high-flying lifestyle set you on a crash course toward financial ruin? Are you moving ahead with no money for retirement? Have your credit card balances snowballed beyond your control? Do you desire financial success—but have no idea where to begin?

In easy-to-understand language, this book explains how you can systematically save—and use those savings to accumulate wealth over time.

You will learn:

✓ How to get out of debt—and stay out
✓ How to use the one surest method for escaping revolving credit card debt
✓ How to set up your own personal program to maximize savings
✓ How to use the best method to multiply your savings many times over
✓ How to develop and achieve your financial goals

✓ How to live below your means—and live happily at the same time

Saving Your Way to Success is the book that can put you solidly on a path to personal and financial success.

Disclaimer

This book is intended to provide accurate information with regard to the subject matter covered. However, the author and publisher accept no responsibility for inaccuracies or omissions, and the author and publisher specifically disclaim any liability, loss, or risk, whether personal, financial, or otherwise, that is incurred as a consequence, directly or indirectly, from the use and/or application of any of the contents of this book.

Praise for Saving Your Way to Success

"*Saving Your Way to Success* is a very practical, user friendly guide to the art, craft, and science of saving money. The informative text is adroitly written for readers of all experience levels, from teenagers saving for college to workers nearing retirement age. *Saving Your Way to Success* is a useful, motivational, no-nonsense book and highly recommended to anyone wanting to enhance their money management skills and secure their personal financial goals.

—Jim Cox,
Midwest Book Review

"(Justin) covers the hows, whys, and results of saving. He does not advocate saving to spend or spending to save, but saving to save as a method to achieving your goals and peace of mind. The advice contained in *Saving Your Way to Success* is well founded and (Justin) speaks from experience. It is sound advice that we can all benefit by."

—Mary Emmons,
eBook Review Weekly

"Want to be a success in life? *Saving Your Way to Success* by Justin addresses the importance of saving money as the key to success.

—David Maack,
The Jamestown Sun

"Anyone interested in saving can follow (Justin's) program which is set out in great detail in *Saving Your Way to Success*. It has been working for him; perhaps it will work for others."

—Jacque Stockman,
Attorney at Law and businessman

Table of Contents

1
WHY SAVE?

*"If you want to know whether you are destined
to be a success or a failure in life, you can easily find out.
The test is simple and it is infallible.
Are you able to save money? If not, drop out. You will lose."*

James J. Hill[1]

Saving is the key to success. There is no other technique available that can generate success for as many people and as powerfully as saving money can. Whether it be minimum wage or a hundred dollars per hour, whether a person is below the poverty line or a multi-millionaire, it makes no difference. Any person can succeed, and saving can create a potential in any person to succeed. Saving makes it possible for any individual, no matter what obstacles present themselves, to successfully reach his or her goals for success. It does not matter what age a person is. It does not matter what obstacles may be impeding the path. It only matters how much income the person is saving to produce success. The person saving nothing will not get ahead, because assets, and thus net worth, will not grow. Income alone does not automatically produce an enormous net worth and success. On the other hand, when saving is done wholeheartedly and passionately, it will bring success. The more a person saves, not earns, the more a person gets ahead. Turn saving money into a highly productive program that will save a lot, and saving becomes the key to success.

Saving can and will unleash the potential inside you to become successful and then make it attainable for you to become rich. The more money you save, the more money you have; thus, you can invest more. If you have more to invest, you have more potential to earn more and a better chance to succeed. Even if you do not invest, by saving more you will increase your net worth dramatically, thus still making you a success. Saving can and will unleash your potential to succeed.

What is Success?

Before you can understand how saving can make you successful, you must first understand the true definition of success.

Too often we consider wealth and fame the things that make a person successful. This assumption is simply not true. Success is not about riches, status, material possessions or income. Quite the opposite—success is about being independent, self-reliant and happy.

Success has a definite purpose. It creates the feeling of accomplishment, satisfaction and happiness all rolled into one package. Success is not about riches, because riches do not necessarily mean independence, self-reliance and happiness. Yes, there are rich people who make a lot of money but are not happy, independent or self-reliant. Success creates within a person the awesome feeling of satisfaction and accomplishment of reaching goals and dreams, of being happy because of it, and of living through a positively rewarding and fulfilling life.

Success is about reaching financial independence. Financial independence is when you are able to dictate your own future because you do not have to rely on others for money. You have no debt or burdening bills. You have no unnecessary loans, but you do have ownership of your possessions. You are not controlled by debt; instead, you have financial control of your life. You will have accumulated a checking account, a savings account and an investment portfolio that together will provide you with a substantial amount of money to counter any disaster, such as a loss of income or home; you will not have to rely on others for money in a time of crisis. This is true success.

When you strive for success in your financial life, you are striving to become financially free. Success and financial freedom are synonymous. When you have accumulated enough savings so you can counter any unexpected expense and handle any disaster that may happen, you have become financially free. When you have become financially free, and no longer need to be dependent on others for financial assistance, and no longer make monthly payments on your house and automobile(s), you have reached true success in life. When you acquire enough money through saving to become financially free, the money worries and problems you were becoming so accustomed to disappear. When you no longer have to worry whether you have enough money to pay the bills, or how you are going to get by, you have become financially free and successful.

Riches do not automatically mean success. They are not synonyms, but are antonyms. Many times a rich person can fall into bankruptcy when a financial disaster appears, including lost income, or a major investment loss. A rich man can just as easily slip on ice and fall down as any other man. It is the same with money. Unless the rich man is as successful as he is rich, he can succumb to failure as easy as the next man.

If one of your neighbors wins a $100,000 lottery, it is a simple fact he has become rich—but has he also become successful? Absolutely not! Five years down the road (or maybe even sooner) while your neighbor has been spending, spending, spending, you have been saving. In those five years, the neighbor's wealth has decreased to nothing, while yours, on the other hand, has proliferated into a monumental sum. If people do not learn how to use and control wealth while they accumulate it, they will not be able to keep it. The neighbor spends all his winnings and in a few years has nothing to show for it; while you, on the other hand, have been living modestly while saving to accumulate your wealth. You will be able to live independently, while the neighbor is stuck back at the level of living paycheck to paycheck, just like he was before winning the lottery. Luxury items or enormous spending do not always mean someone is successful; rather, they may only mean the person is a spender not a saver—he or she does not know how to handle money.

Lasting happiness never comes from money. It comes from the dignity and self-satisfaction of being able to stand tall because you have accomplished your goals and dreams, have become self-reliant and self-supportive, and have become financially independent for the rest of your life. Happiness will come from success; it will not come from money.

"Happiness is found in doing, not merely in possessing," wrote Napoleon Hill[2]. By becoming successful, by doing, by accomplishing your goals, you will be happy. Possessions never bring long lasting, true happiness; rather, they only bring short-lived, forgettable happiness. Happiness comes from accomplishing something, whether it is to become successful, to create a wonderful piece of art, to fix a problem, or to change another person's attitude through your own positive personality. Long lasting, veritable happiness will never come from material possessions.

Wealth is the Culmination of Success Through Saving

After reaching the awesome triumph of success, you can continue forward to reach wealth. Riches do not necessarily come with success, and most of the time will not come before success; but once success is reached, as long as you desire riches and endeavor to get them, you are almost guaranteed that the riches will come.

In fact, many people want success so they will have wealth and fame. There is nothing wrong with desiring wealth and then having wealth. Becoming rich may even be the culmination of your successful life. *The problem is some people want wealth before success.* Wealth may come, but without success firmly set in place, the wealth may disappear as quickly as it appeared. Someone who acquired wealth without the hard, vigorous work, time, and effort will not have the savvy to retain his or her wealth because there was little invested in acquiring that wealth. Wealth is not a prerequisite of success, but if a successful person desires wealth, wealth will be his or hers.

The goal of this book, *Saving Your Way to Success*, is not exclusively to procure you wealth; rather, the goal is to explain and describe how saving money, a constant and consistent desire of success, and vigorous work toward your goals will be the key to helping you reach the success you desire. Do not expect wealth to come automatically, but do expect wealth to come after

4

you have reached success, if you desire to continue forward and acquire it.

How can you succeed by saving? It seems simple: develop a habit to save a portion of what you earn every month. "An augmentation of fortune is the means by which the greater part of men propose and wish to better their condition. It is the means the most vulgar and the most obvious; and the most likely way of augmenting their fortune, is to save and accumulate some part of what they acquire... regularly and annually," wrote Adam Smith.[3] Saving can make you rich—first by turning you into a successfully independent, self-reliant, proud individual and secondly, by creating the opportunity for wealth because you have become successful through saving.

Rich is nice, but success is better. It does not take a lot of money to become successful, and success is what makes acquiring wealth possible. To become rich, become successful first—by incorporating thriftiness into your life. *Saving is the key to success, and success is the key to wealth.*

Overcome the Obstacles to Save

Why save? Will not working longer and/or investing be enough to become successful and ultimately richer? Certainly, working more hours will get you a bigger paycheck, and investing more may get you a bigger return on your investments—but these are not the key. To become successful safely and securely without the fatigue and soreness of long, tedious workdays and without the stress and risks of a multitude of investments, *save*. Planned saving can get you a better reward much more easily than long work and risky investments. Certainly, investing money and working hard also help you to become a success; but to succeed much more quickly and safely, saving should be firmly in place as the key ingredient.

If saving is so great, why do not a majority of people save? There are several reasons: Many people think of saving as being miserly, as hoarding money. Some insist that taxes and inflation would eat up their savings. Others blame their "inability" to save on unrelated irrelevant excuses—in reality, they can save if they would just put their minds to it. It is very common that those who do not save are compulsive spenders; they would rather have instant gratification from buying something instead of saving their way to success.

The problem with all these excuses for not saving money is they miss the single most important reason to save money—reaching success. A person may have to overcome obstacles to save money: misconceptions of the consequences, not knowing how to save, debt, or a small income. These are all detriments, but as soon as you start to save money, these obstacles are soon removed. Some people say they have too little income and too many expenses. In reality those same people probably have upper class incomes they spend on luxury items they consider "necessary expenses"—luxury automobiles, expensive attire, and a maid to clean the house. Saving *eliminates* the problems of inadequate income and over burdening expenses. If you are delaying your savings program due to low income, and/or high debt and/or enormous expenses, you are missing *the* reason to save. If you begin saving via a thrifty lifestyle you will eliminate burdening debt and expenses while at the same time increasing income and net worth.

Take the initiative. Stop complaining and start doing. Develop a personal savings program and begin to automatically save a portion of every paycheck. Develop a plan to save money, save substantial amounts of money, and work on the plan every day.

Misconceptions about Saving

To unleash the potential of enormous savings, you do not need to even consider becoming a miser. A person could not survive in today's business climate by being a miser, but by saving, or being frugal, you can survive and grow besides. Thrift will become a part of your lifestyle when you save your way to success, but just because you are savvy with your money does not mean you will have to live as a miserable miser. On the contrary, you will live with excitement as you overcome obstacles, save more and more, and move closer to success. To enjoy the fruits of your labor excessive stinginess does not necessarily have to become a part of your life—but you do need to begin to save a sizable amount (maybe as much as 50%) of your income.

When you begin to save your way to success, you will need to become thrifty and diligent with your money. Yes, it is requisite you change your habits from a spender's to a saver's lifestyle. Yes, this means, for awhile, you will not be able to buy as many things because your spending will be dramatically decreased. No, all of this will not create misery. When you begin to move ahead, accomplish goals, and turn obstacles into achievements, the slight discomfort of reducing your wants will not feel like misery, but will feel like success.

Saving Correctly

Saving can do a lot for you when you do it correctly, consistently, and exploit it to its fullest. Success through saving comes about when you save correctly by doing these things:

- Maximizing your savings.
- Create a plan to save a portion of every paycheck.
- Constantly think "save" rather than "spend."

You do not save to buy something, such as a car; rather, you are saving toward success. Meager savings is why many people believe there are no rewards to saving. The rewards come when you begin to save correctly. When you begin to maximize your savings you are not hoarding money, or living in misery because you cannot buy anything; rather, you are saving toward your personal success. When you begin to save correctly you will begin reaping the genuine rewards.

What is meant by saving correctly? You must save more than just a measly 5 or 10 percent. In 1997 the *New York Times* reported the U.S. savings rate had plunged to 3.8% of income, which at the time was a 58-year low.[4] In 2001, the national savings rate plunged even further as Americans saved a pathetic 1.6% of disposable income.[5] *Saving Your Way to Success* will show how you can be above average. This is not saving, this is just putting aside what is left over. True saving is when you max out—saving 40 to 50% or up to as much as 80% under certain circumstances.

To save correctly, you must think "save" rather than "spend." "The word *saving* has come to mean "spending" in our society. People are fooled into thinking they are saving money when they are in fact, spending it. For example, a housewife will buy a new household appliance because it was advertised with the words, 'Buy now and save $49 off the regular price!' You do not save money by spending. Then there is the man who subscribes to the bank's 'Christmas Savings Plan' to save money for Christmas shopping. That is not a plan for saving—it is a plan for spending." wrote George M. Bowman.[6] When you save money only in order to spend your money, you are not saving your way to success.

Saving money to buy an expensive item does not help you reach success. Once the expensive stereo, car, or fancy dress is bought, the money is gone. True saving is when you keep your money, become richer, increase your assets and net worth, and then become a success because of it.

If you spend all your money, how do you expect to become successful? Maybe you will win the lottery, but unless you are extremely auspicious, do not count on it. There is a better system with much more favorable odds of up to a 100% guarantee. That system is saving. Save your money and you will become successful.

Save or Spend

When you earn money, you have two options on what to do with it: save or spend. If you spend it, it is gone. If you save it, you still have it and can then invest it. Most people choose to spend most of their money. Only a select few, through prudence

8

and perception, save a majority of the money they earn. If more is saved, more can be invested, and a bigger return can be the reward.

Saving comes about when you earn money and decide not to spend it. It is that simple. There are no other options. You can either be a spender or a saver.

To reach success through saving, you will need to start basing your buying (and non-buying) decisions on the need to save money all the time in order to maximize your savings. If you still make decisions that are costing you money and keeping you from reaching your maximum savings, you will not be able to reach success as quickly as you could—if you reach it at all. To save your way to success you need to always think "save" and base not just your money decisions, but all of your decisions, on the fact that you desire to save your way to success.

Investing

Investing is an important ingredient to increasing your wealth and reaching success. A savings account and certificate of deposits (CDs) pay only nominal interest, but if you would like to see your money grow at a rate that will possibly make you a multi-millionaire, then you should be investing.

Investing must become an ingredient of your personal plan to become a success. Smart, savvy, long-term investing allows your savings to grow at a much faster compounding rate than from saving alone. Your money needs the magic of compounding working for you to accumulate a substantial amount of wealth.

Would you rather have your money growing at 12% annual compounded growth rate, which is the historical growth rate for a solid, long-term mutual fund invested in the United States stock market, or would you rather be earning only 6% in a CD?

The following example explains the magic of compounding assuming you save $2,000 only one time and have 42 years until you retire:

Rule of 72: 72 / yearly rate of growth = number of years for your money to double.

Years Invested	72 / 6% = 12	or 72 / 12% = 6.
6 years		$4,000
12 years	$4,000	$8,000
18 years		$16,000
24 years	$8,000	$32,000
30 years		$64,000
36 years	$16,000	$128,000
42 years	$24,000	$256,000

By the time you retire, if you invested only $2,000 in the stock market and earned an average of 12% annual compounded interest, your money would have doubled 7 times into an amazing $256,000! Compare this to only $24,000—what your money would have grown to in the CD. The magic of compounding is astounding!

What would you rather have—10 million dollars, or only 1 penny that doubled every day for 31 days?

Think about this for a moment. The answer is astounding.

I hope you choose the 1 penny that doubled every day for 31 days, because that penny would have multiplied into $10,737,418.24!

The compounding of your money is worth far more than any lottery or prize you could win. Rather than waiting for your luck "to turn for the better" and for you to win the lottery, you could begin sacrificing a little bit and investing now; therefore, over the long term you will accumulate your own winning lottery ticket in the form of a multi-million dollar investment portfolio.

Investing is an essential ingredient to reaching the financial prosperity you desire. Saving is the key to getting out of debt, reducing your bills and financial worries and the key to success, but if you really desire your money to grow, you must invest your money. Once you have established your savings program and have about 6 month's to 1 year's worth of income in a savings account, it is time for you to begin investing.

As with saving, the longer you procrastinate with investing, the less you will be able to accumulate. Consider the following example. John Frugal starts investing in the stock market at age 25 and continues to do so until age 65. He invests $200 a month consistently and on time every month for the next forty years. His invested money totals $96,000, but at an average 9% annual compounded interest, his investment has grown to $850,000! William Spendall, on the other hand, procrastinates and does not implement an investment program until the age of 45. He invests $400 per month for 20 years until he also retires at the age of 65. His total investment is also $96,000, but at the same 9% annual compounded interest, his investment has grown to only $257,000. William lacked time perspective. John had the self-discipline to sacrifice only $200 a month early in his life to have greater prosperity when he retired.

John Frugal	William Spendall
$200 a month	$400 a month
Invested from age 25 to age 65	Invested from age 45 to age 65
$96,000 total investment	$96,000 total investment
9% annual compounded interest	9% annual compounded interest
= $850,000 total wealth accumulation	= $257,000 total wealth accumulation

If you are climbing out of debt, beginning your savings program, or still accumulating an amount to counter a financial disaster or problem, then you need to wait before you begin investing. Once you are well on your way to getting out of debt and saving your way to success, give yourself a boost by first learning how to invest, and then investing some of your saved money.

To invest you first must save. The more money you save the more money you have to invest. If you were saving 10% of your earnings, and investing all of the 10%, then begin saving 20%, the new 10% can be invested or not. Saving comes first. Then you must invest your savings wisely to make your savings work and grow for you to earn you a greater return on your money.

Work Alone Will not Bring Success

Many people think work alone will make you successful—an idea as erroneous as that of becoming a miser if you save. Work by itself earns money, but saving is what creates success.

Money earned from work must be saved, and not spent. If it is spent, than the extra work did not make you richer or more successful. If the extra money earned from extra work is not saved, then nothing was accomplished. By saving extra earned money from extra work, you will be moving forward. Extra work alone will not do much, except make you more hungry and tired, but with savings it can make you more successful and richer. Work is the key to making money, but saving is the key to success. Few people understand the power of hard work plus saving.

Throughout this book you will find out how two exactly opposite friends, John Frugal and William Spendall, make saving versus spending decisions that affect their lives. You too can decide to either be a saver or a spender with each decision you make, and each decision of your life is based on your and their own personalities, which is either a spender or a saver.

As you read Saving Your Way to Success pay careful attention to the examples of John Frugal and William Spendall. With every example stop and think for a moment, "Which one of these two am I, which one do I want to be?" Maybe before reading this book you would have done many of the things William Spendall has done without even realizing they are affecting your savings.

John Frugal and William Spendall

Let us look at two friends, young adults who are exact opposites. John Frugal is the saver, who desires, plans, and works towards success. William Spendall is also a good person and a hard worker, who dreams of success. William rarely works toward his goals; rather, he wants success to simply fall into his lap. These two friends are perfect examples of what saving versus spending is all about. One will certainly become successful. The other will only dream of success.

During the summer, William Spendall makes $1,500 every two weeks because he is a hard worker. He puts in lots of overtime and likes bringing home a nice big check. John Frugal also makes $1,500 every two weeks, because John is also a hard worker. They work at the same place and earn the same wage. At the end of the summer the two friends are out of a job. After a few weeks, William Spendall wants to borrow money from John Frugal. John does not need to borrow, and does not want to lend money to William. Why? They both worked hard and earned the same amount of money. They should have the same amount of money, but they do not. Why does William Spendall have to borrow while John does not need to borrow at all? William Spendall worked hard and earned lots of money, but as soon as he is out of work, William is also out of money, because he did not save. John Frugal, also out of work, still has money, and can be earning money on his money because he saved. John Frugal is successful; William Spendall is not—a classic example of how saving and work, together, will make you a success.

Remember three key economic sentences:

- Work is not the key to success.
- Work is the key to making money.
- Making more money and saving your money are the keys to success.

Working hard will earn you money. Working harder will earn you more money. It does not matter how hard you work and how much you earn, unless you save it. You may be able to afford new clothes, or get a newer car, or eat at classy restaurants, but you are not getting ahead in relationship to success.

"Hard work is the best investment a man can make," Charles M. Schwab, an American steel manufacturer, stated inspirationally in 1931[7]. Hard work needs to be a part of your plan to achieving success. Working hard helps you get ahead; it is a very wise investment.

In order to save money you need to earn money. The harder you work, the more money you can earn, the more you can save and the more imminent success becomes. It works in that sequence. Scramble it out of order and it leaves you with nothing. Work in itself will not make you a success, but working harder to earn more money, to save more money will. The only place where success comes before work is in the dictionary.

When working harder and longer to earn more, you must also work and think smarter. Rather than hiring someone who can work sixty hours a week, would not most employers hire an employee who can do the same amount of work in forty hours by working smarter and harder. Employers will hire, praise, and promote employees who can do sixty hours of work in forty hours, saving employers money. In fact, the employer now has more money which he may decide to give some or all to the better employee as in profit sharing or some other benefit in return for the extra hard work. Elbert Hubbard, an American editor and writer, was quoted with an inspirational statement on work: "Folks who never do any more than what they get paid for, never get paid for any more than they do."[8] Pay heed to Elbert Hubbard's quote and you will move a step close to success.

Which is better? Working sixty hours to earn eight hundred dollars, or working forty hours to earn the same amount—or maybe even only seven hundred dollars, but having an extra twenty hours to earn more and save more from other work, such as a second income? By working smarter and not longer, you have saved yourself not only money, but time and energy as well.

How have you saved money? Those extra twenty hours can now be used to bring in more earnings which can be saved. You have also saved yourself from overworking, which can put you out of work. Working harder is extremely beneficial—but if working harder and longer over a long period of time forces you to miss work, then you have lost those earnings and potential savings. Working in itself can not possibly make you more successful; it will only earn you money. Working harder and smarter, being frugal with your money, and saving and investing wisely will make you successful.

Saving and work must be brought together for success. Work harder and smarter to earn more money. After more money is earned you will be able to save more money. With more money saved, you will be able to reap the benefits of success through saving much sooner. Invest in yourself to use your time and effort to increase the knowledge you have of your career. Work wholeheartedly and ingeniously to prove to your boss you go the extra mile and deserve the raise. By saving and working smarter and harder, you will be able to reach success.

John Frugal and William spendall

Let us return to our two opposite friends, William Spendall and John Frugal. William Spendall has earned $50 today, but has a chance to earn another $20. Since he is a hard worker, and wants to work longer to make more, William takes the opportunity. He now has $70—but pays the car repair bill of $30, and has $40 left.

John Frugal also has $50, but does not take the opportunity to work extra and earn extra. John is working smarter. Instead of the extra work, John fixes the car himself. (Doing things yourself is a great money saving technique.) By fixing the car himself, John is saving $30 that would have gone to the car repair shop. He still has $50, $10 more than William. John Frugal has worked smarter and earned more by saving.

Benefits of Saving

"Capitals are increased by parsimony, and diminished by prodigality and misconduct," wrote Adam Smith.[9] *To increase your capital and purchasing power you do not need more money; you just need to save.* By saving on the car repair bill, John Frugal increased his capital by ten dollars. John also increased his purchasing power by saving when buying an item at one dollar instead of two dollars; he had another dollar which could be used to buy something else if the need or want was there. John increased his earnings through saving. William Spendall, by spending rather than saving, did not. This is what saving can do for you. By first saving twice as much—by saving when you earn and then saving when you buy—you will increase your capital and purchasing power. Following that, you will increase your net worth, reach goals and dreams, and then ultimately get ahead and reach success—and if you want, wealth thereafter.

Saving can do all this and much more when you desire to use it effectively. Plan to save and plan to succeed. Stop spending and begin saving. Increase your earning power through more saving. You can increase your capital and purchasing power without working many long hours or taking risky investments. If you start early the potential of your savings can be huge. With determination, you can do it.

Why should you start saving? Take a look at the following chart. It explains why you should not just plan to save, but start saving immediately. Compare the fifth year of your savings of $3,600.53 ($50 per month at 7% interest compounded monthly) to forty years after beginning your monthly savings. By the fortieth year, your savings will have grown to $132,006.24. Start saving now!

You need to start saving immediately! If you wait only five years, you will be drastically reducing your total accumulation. As you examine the chart, "Why Should You Start Saving Now?" take notice of the significant difference between 40 years of saving and 45 years of saving. If you were to save $200 a month for 45 years (earning 7% interest compounded monthly) your total accumulation would equal almost $763,000! If you wait only five years to start saving, those five years of lost compounding equal a greatly reduced total accumulation. By saving $200 a month for only 40 years, you accumulate $235,000 less than if you started saving five years earlier. The magic of compounding over long periods is what turns $200 a month saved into over a quarter of a million dollars! This is why you should start saving now.

Why Should You Start Saving Now?

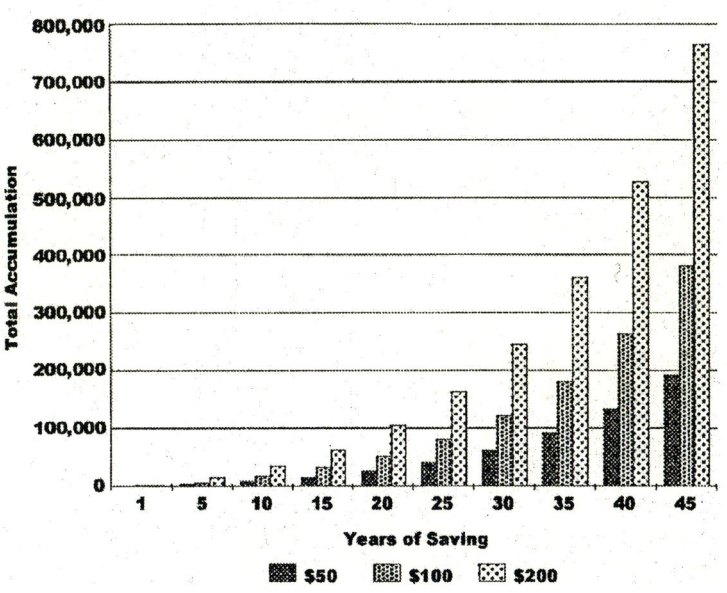

Saving will make you financially sound, and may make you richer; and, most importantly, it will make you self-reliant, financially free, and independent. "My glass is not large, but I drink from *my* glass," said the French writer Alfred De Musset (emphasis added).[10] Your glass will be yours, and it will be paid for. You will not have to take government hand-outs and rely on others to support you, because you will be standing tall and proud of your achievement of sound financial status. You will be successful. Saving will keep you out of beggary, spending will not. Samuel Smiles explains it: "He who spends all he gets is on his way to beggary."[11] Do not spend your way to the poor house; rather, save your way to independence. You may not be rich, but you will be financially secure.

When done correctly, saving will make you financially sound. You may not be rich, but you will be independent. You may not have the things the neighbor will be paying interest on for many years to come, but you will have your own things and they will be paid completely for. You will not have all those interest payments, credit card payments, car and house payments that add up to a pile of debt. You will be standing on your own two feet; you will be financially independent and successful. You may not have the fanciest, but you will always have it. You will not have any obligatory debts, be controlled by someone else who pulls your financial strings, or be bankrupt. You will be successfully independent and know that you put yourself there with your own hands, mind and perseverance. That is success.

Saving will force you to be a responsible individual. Whether you have a big bank account or a small one, you will be successful because all your bills are paid for. If you work hard, continue to learn more, learn from your experiences, and really desire it, you will become successful. You will be able to be proud of your financial achievements. Henry David Thoreau, wrote: "If one advances confidently in the direction of his dreams, and endeavors to live the life which he has imagined, he will meet with a success unexpected in common hours." He continued, "If you have built castles in the air, your work need not be lost; that is where they should be. Now put the foundations under them."[12] You have the dreams, the castles. Build the foundations. Build those dreams into realities. It will not happen until you begin. Yes, you can do it. Plan to save; plan to succeed!

Points to Ponder:

- Success is not about riches, status, material possessions, or income. Quite the opposite; success is about being independent, self-reliant, and happy.
- A person may have to overcome obstacles to save money, including misconceptions of the consequence of saving money, or the obstacles of ignorance, or debt, or too small of an income; but, an obstacle is not a failure, it is only a small pothole in the road of success.
- Correct saving means when you save you use your money to become successful rather than using it foolishly like buying a new car, stereo, or some other fancy material item.
- You have only two choices. If you spend, you cannot save; but if you do not spend, then you are saving.
- Work is not the key to success; but without hard work, success will not be possible. In order to save money you need to earn money. The harder and more efficiently you work, the more money you can earn, the more you can save and the closer to success you become.
- If you spend all your money, how do you expect to become successful? Maybe you will win the lottery; but, unless you are extremely lucky, do not count on it. There is a better system with much more favorable odds—nearly a 100% guarantee. That system is saving. Save your money, and you will become successful.
- Like John Frugal and William Spendall, you can decide to be either a saver or a spender. Each decision is based on your own personality—that of a spender or a saver—and each and every decision you make affects your drive to success.
- Saving will first and foremost make you a success; but, it will also increase your capital and purchasing power, and in the end it can and will make you rich.

Plan to save; plan to succeed.

2
Reach for Your Savings Potential

"There are no limitations except those you acknowledge. Whatever you can conceive and believe, you can achieve."

Napoleon Hill[1]

On a clear night, count the stars in the sky. They represent how many ways people, sometimes unknowingly, save money. Now imagine how many stars there are up there you cannot see. Those are all the possibilities there are to save.

The next time at the beach, begin counting all the pebbles there are around you. They represent how many ways people save. Then stand up and take in the enormity of how many pebbles there could be on the entire beach. Those are all the savings possibilities most people do not know about.

Does this make saving impossible? On the contrary, it makes saving so much easier! With so many possibilities for saving it is possible for you to save all the time—maybe even without knowing that you are saving. The more ways there are to save the more chances you will have to reach your full savings potential.

With such a multitude of possibilities, no one who wants to reach success through saving will have an excuse for not saving money most, if not, all of the time. And the more possibilities you find for saving, the more money you can save during a given time, and the better chance you will have for reaching the success you desire.

There are countless possibilities for saving money. Any and every time you earn and spend, you have the chance to save money. Once you master the formula for saving, you can start saving virtually all the time.

John Frugal and William Spendall

Over a month, our two opposite friends, John Frugal and William Spendall, decide to compare notes on how they advanced toward their goals for success. Both dream of success and becoming rich someday—but John works vigorously toward his goal by mastering the key to success, which is saving, while William does not. Over the past month, John had a clear advantage over William in his reach for success. William had only saved money in 25% of the instances where he had purchased something. John, on the other hand, had saved nearly 75% of the time he purchased something. At the end of the month, John had accumulated almost three times as much money from saving as William had. John Frugal was using all the money saving methods and techniques he could in order to maximize his savings potential. Over a period of a few years, John will build his savings portfolio to such a degree it will enable him to reach financial freedom years before William can even think of reaching such a goal.

Like John Frugal, you too must use all of the money saving methods, ideas, and techniques that you can in order for you to maximize your savings.

Save as Much as You Desire

With so many ways to save, a person can save up to 50% of his or her earnings—and more! Reaching a savings rate of 50% of your net income (gross income minus taxes and social security) may seem dramatic, or unreachable, or unrealistic, but if you are willing to work vigorously and wholeheartedly to reach success, 50% is a very attainable number. Most people can attain a 25 to 50% savings, but for a select few the savings level can reach 80%. Impossible? Hardly! It does take a few specific circumstances, but it is possible (we will explain these in a later chapter). For now, for most of us, a 25 to 50% savings level is an achievable goal.

Why should you save as much as you can? The following chart has the answer. Compare the first number of $50 monthly savings to $500 or even $1,000 monthly savings. At a 5% interest (compounded monthly), $50 saved a month accumulates to only $76,618.93 in 40 years. $500 a month saved is able to grow to a whopping $766,189.29 at the same 5% compounded monthly interest. And $1,000 mushrooms to more than $1.5 million! This is why you should reach for your savings potential.

Why You Should Save as Much as You Can

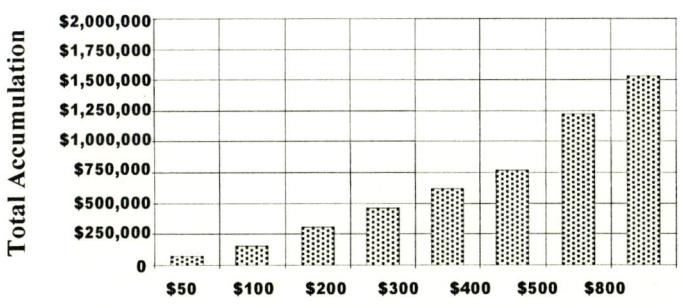

Savings Per Month

The chart, "Why You Should Save as Much as You Can," elucidates the money saving fact—the more money you can save now, the greater wealth accumulation you will have in your future. By simply reaching for your maximum savings potential—maybe as much as $1,000 per month—rather than only saving a small minimum—$50 per month—you will multiply your retirement wealth by as much as 10 or 20 fold!

You may or may not be in the position to save 50% of your take home pay, but you can still save much more than you are. In 1996, Americans saved an average of only 4.3%.[2] Only 4.3%! Where is all the other income going? Overall household debt grew to 89% of disposable income in 1996, a sharp increase over 1980's figure of 67%.[3] In 1997, the savings rate continued to drop. The *New York Times* reported the U.S. savings rate had plunged to 3.8% of income, a 58-year low.[4] In 2001, the national savings rate plunged even further as Americans saved a pathetic

1.6% of disposable income.[5] Turn 4% into 40%—an amazing ten-fold increase!

How I Did It

How do I know a 50% savings rate is achievable? It is because I accomplished it. Over a set period of one year, I maintained a precisely accurate, yet simple and concise, record. I tested and analyzed the methods which are explained throughout this book to prove they will save money. All expenses and incomes were included. During that year I was able to consistently save over 50% of my take home pay. In four out of the twelve months the numbers added up to less than 50%, but the average of the twelve months was over 57%! I was not able to attain a 50% savings rate every month, but through persistence and desire to reach the goal, and the willingness to work wholeheartedly in reaching it, I was easily able to reach beyond my goal of a total 50% savings rate for the twelve months.

How was I able to do this? You may think I had a special set of circumstances, but I assure you I did not. I only had an average hourly wage. I had bills to pay like everyone else: I had rent, electricity, and food. I was not getting any free necessities.

The only special circumstance which aided me in my quest was that I had no dependents. Still, even if you are the bread winner of your family, you and the rest of your family can drastically increase your savings rate to surprising figures. You may or may not be able to reach a 50% savings rate, but by following the guidelines described throughout *Saving Your Way to Success*, you will be able to reach your fullest savings potential. No matter what your circumstances, you can save your way to success.

My first step was to create an income and expense record book. If you desire to reach your maximum savings potential you should have your own record book (to be discussed in detail in chapter 7). Keep track of everything, and it will become an indispensable tool allowing you to calculate how much you are saving, show you how you can improve your savings, disclose to you what expenses are eating away most of your money, prove you are reaching your goals, and help you create new goals. Keeping this record helped me reach and surpass my goals; it can do the same for you.

My first test was one of the months I was unable to reach a savings rate of 50%. Amazingly, however, it was during the same month I moved out of my parents' home—and still saved 35% of my income. We all know there is some added expense when a person moves, but to top it off I had to furnish many things, including a television, recliner, a few pots and pans, new phone and utility accounts, and one month's rent after paying the deposit the previous month. How did I manage to do all this and save? The key factor, which will be explained in more detail in later sections of the book, was that I bought perfectly good *used* furniture and appliances. At the end of the month I knew I would easily reach and surpass my goal of 50% in month two.

As the second month of the test ended, I learned the hard way that things do not turn out the way you intended; yet, I was still able to save 51%, just enough to surpass my goal. I was satisfied because I reached my goal, but I knew I could do better.

Over the next two months I saw myself increase my savings rate to 62% for each month. My income increased to approximately the same size as it was the first month, but my savings also increased as much. I was now settled down in my apartment. I had no more "extra" bills for hook-ups or furniture. By following the methods described throughout this book, I was able to save nearly two-thirds of my income. I was simply amazed. I still had money to have fun, despite saving such a large percentage of my income.

Why the variations in income? I had a regular, full-time job and I would take on extra work including raking and mowing lawns, small maintenance and repair jobs, or anything else in which I was proficient. I became caretaker of a small apartment building, plus I had the eagerness to work overtime on my regular job when the chance arose. This second income increased my total income anywhere from between 8 to 33% with an average of 19.86%. By earning a second income, I was able to increase my total income by 20%, while simultaneously increasing my savings by the same amount because I did not spend any portion of the extra income. By increasing my income by 20% per month I guaranteed my success in reaching the savings rate I desired.

During the remaining months, my savings would increase or decrease in direct proportion to an increase or decrease in income. When I was able to generate a larger income, I did not spend more; I only saved more toward my success. My lowest monthly income was only $1,200—and I was still able to save substantially over 50%.

There was only a single month in which I was unable to reach a 50% savings. During this month I had to pay a six-month premium for liability automobile insurance. Being a male, and under age 25 at the time, I found car insurance unbelievably expensive. I should have split this expense into an even amount for each of the six months, but I wanted to see if I could reach a 50% savings rate. Through hard work, desire, and persistence I was still able to come close to my goal of 50%, with a 46.5% savings rate.

After the last month, and after calculating the specifics I knew I now had tested proven methods which will allow almost anyone to save 50%. Several keys to remember are:

1. I bought no new furniture. Everything was purchased used and it was in good to excellent shape.
2. I used all the methods to save money on food when the opportunity was there. One excellent method which helped save money was a garden I aided my parents in cultivating.
3. I had more than one income.
4. I did my own maintenance and repair on my older, used automobile, a 1982 Plymouth Grand Fury, whenever it was possible. (By the way, I purchased this mechanically good car for only $100!)
5. I had no one else but myself to take care of. I was completely independent in my living (This in no way implies that with a family you will not be able to maximize your savings).
6. I developed a plan through which I automatically deducted a portion of money whenever I received money and placed it

into a savings account, therefore automatically limiting how much I could spend.

Every one of these methods played a significant role in allowing me to reach a savings rate of 57.22% for the twelve months.

You, too, can reach your savings potential by following the proven methods described throughout *Saving Your Way to Success*. Every person has a different maximum savings potential. Maybe you are the spouse who supports the family, and a 50% savings rate may not be reached—but you can still reach your maximum potential, even if it is less. Maximum potential means reaching the greatest savings rate possible under your specific conditions. Some people, under specific conditions (as will be elucidated in chapter six), can save as much as 80%. You may or may not be one of those people, but you can still reach your savings potential. Become more than just an average person—save more than just 4 or 5%. Set a goal of what you want to save, start working toward your goal and you will reach it.

How much can you save? It really only matters how much you are willing to work, use your time, and sacrifice. The amount is unlimited. Do you desire 25%? Work towards your goal ardently and you will easily achieve your goal. If you want to save more, because you desire success to come sooner, set a goal of 50% or more. Start working toward your goal immediately, follow the proven methods in this book, desire to reach your goal sincerely and work with as much discipline as necessary to reach your goal.

Motivating Yourself to Succeed

As long as there is a desire to reach a goal, the goal can be accomplished, and by saving over and over again, you will habituate yourself to saving. When it becomes second nature, you are guaranteed success through saving.

To do this, you must invest in yourself. By investing in yourself, you will discipline yourself to use your time and effort constantly and persistently and work toward your goal every day, remaining enthusiastic in what you do each day, learning new ways of how you can save, and continuing to desire to reach your goal.

How do you invest in *you*? Use your enthusiasm and desire to discipline yourself to learn as much as you can, to use your effort and time wisely, and to work ardently toward your goals. Until you have invested in yourself, you will be missing the key ingredients needed to reach any goal: desire, work, discipline, knowledge, time, effort and enthusiasm.

DESIRE

You must have desire to reach any goal. Napoleon Hill wrote: "When *desire* focuses you toward your victory, you do not need any way to retreat, victory is certain."[6] When you desire success, rather than just wish for it, you are telling your subconscious mind you must reach success. When your mind, the greatest computer you have, acknowledges this, it will do everything possible to acquire success. When you desire something so much your desire programs your mind into actually believing you must have it to survive, it will create ideas and plans that will allow you to get what you have been programming your mind to get. There is no possibility of failure.

WHOLEHEARTED WORK

A person who works wholeheartedly, constantly and persistently, toward a desired result will get the desired result. The person who works only half-heartedly will only get half-hearted results—and will never reach savings goals. A person who does not persistently and constantly work toward a goal will falter in the end.

Your work should be a labor of love, not just a means to draw a paycheck. The more work you put into something, the more constant and persistent time and effort you put into something, the better end result. Unless you only want half-success, you must work wholeheartedly towards success.

DISCIPLINE

Without discipline you will not be able to change yourself into what you want to be. You must have the discipline to control the urge to stray from the drive toward the goal, or the urge to quit the drive altogether.

Discipline yourself to stay on the proper paths that will lead to success. As soon as you waiver in your discipline of saving money, your potential to reach success will decline. Discipline yourself to reduce the many wants—not needs—you are buying. Discipline yourself to use coupons when buying something. Discipline yourself to remove an obstacle, such as an addiction. Discipline yourself to follow your program of saving. Discipline yourself into believing you can reach success through your desire for success.

KNOWLEDGE

"If a man empties his purse into his head, no man can take it away from him," Benjamin Franklin stated. "An investment in knowledge, always pays the best interest."[7] Knowledge is the best investment a person can make. By reading *Saving You Way to Success*, and continuing to learn and read, you will develop the capabilities for reaching success. A sagacious saver is a saver who will be able to maximize his or her potential.

Without learning how to reach success, you will not be able to reach success. You must acquire knowledge in order to do something. If you do not know how to save money, you will not be able to. If you do not know saving is the key to success, you will not be able to reach success through saving. By acquiring new knowledge, you will be able to do more, accomplish more, understand more, be better at what you do, and reach success.

TIME and EFFORT

How much you can save is directly proportional to how much effort and time you are willing to sacrifice. The more you are willing to do to get results, the better results you get. When you were a student, or if you are a student, you know you normally get better grades on the tests for which you put more time and effort into studying. The same goes for saving toward your success. If you desire a 50% savings rate, use all your effort and time and work wholeheartedly toward your goal, you will reach it, no matter what your circumstances are.

An anonymous maxim is, "Count that day lost whose low descending sun views from thy hand no worthy action done." Always do something at least once a day which is going to help you reach your savings goal. Use every day to reach for your goals of success, and you will become closer to reaching those goals everyday.

ENTHUSIASM

Unless you have the enthusiasm to work, to change, to learn, to use your effort and time, you will not do it. You must have intense zeal for acquiring success to be able to acquire it. "I am convinced that the fortunate individuals who achieve the most in life are invariably activated by enthusiasm," Norman Vincent Peale wrote, "The men who do the most with their lives are those who approach human existence, its opportunities and its problems—even its rough moments—with a confident attitude and an enthusiastic point of view."[8]

Desire and enthusiasm are closely related, but still distinctly different. When you wish for something earnestly you desire it. If you are intensely eager and hopeful in getting something, you are enthusiastic. A person must desire success enthusiastically in order to reach success. Both are needed. If you are enthusiastic about reaching success, but do not desire it, you will never reach success, because all you will be doing is *thinking* about success. You will only be interested in reaching success, not desiring to *work* to reach it. One ingredient missing will destroy the results of the recipe. Enthusiastic desire will propel you to your dreams and goals.

If any one of these ingredients is missing in yourself, you have not fully invested in your best weapon—yourself. If you are not ready, not fully vested in your drive for success, how do you expect to reach success? A good dish needs all the ingredients a recipe requires. In saving your way to success you must first invest in your own personality, changing it, if need be, so you can reach success. Just reading Saving Your Way to Success will not breed success. You must take newly acquired knowledge from this book and begin to use it. Use *enthusiastic desire* to *discipline* yourself to *work wholeheartedly* with all your *time and effort* constantly and persistently. Invest in yourself, your most valuable asset, your most powerful weapon, your greatest tool, and you will be able to reach whatever goals you set.

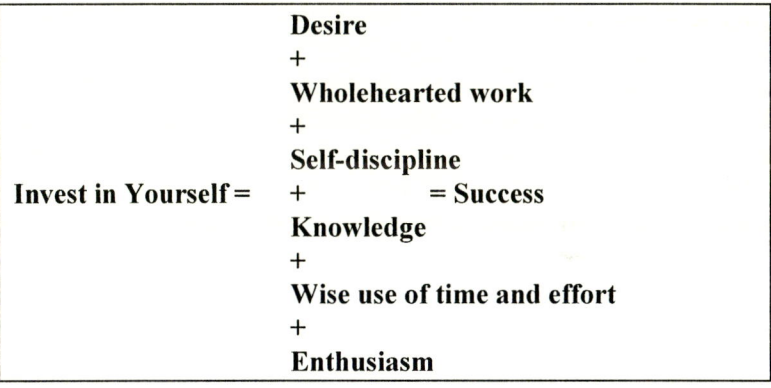

	Desire	
	+	
	Wholehearted work	
	+	
	Self-discipline	
Invest in Yourself =	+	**= Success**
	Knowledge	
	+	
	Wise use of time and effort	
	+	
	Enthusiasm	

Know the Formulas to Save All the Time

Once you have decided to invest in yourself, you will find there are thousands of ways to save. With so many ways to save, how can anyone learn all of them? To even begin to explain all the possibilities on how to save would take an encyclopedia-like format. So much time would probably be spent learning ways to save that the savings would not be worth it.

The good news is an encyclopedia is unnecessary. Instead, all you need to know are the formulas for saving. *Saving Your*

Way to Success will give you the formulas for saving all the time. You do not need to know the answers to every mathematical problem; you need only the formulas so you can solve each problem as it appears before you.

To know how to save every time you do not need to go through every circumstance that might occur; you need only know how to save every time so you do not have to deal with circumstantial variables. There may be hundreds of ways you can save when you buy one specific item. You can save by buying when the item is on sale, or using a coupon or rebate, or buying used or bulk, or buying non-brand and more. If you combine even two of these methods, you now have a new way to save.

How can you possibly memorize how to save with all these methods and so many things you spend your money on? The answer is you do not have to. You only need to know the methods themselves. Do not memorize ways to save—instead, learn how to save!

To explain in a single book all the possibilities of how to save we only need to consolidate those possiblities into savings methods. You will not learn how to save on a few select items, but you will learn to save every time on everything under all kinds of circumstances. Rather than memorizing the problem and the answer, you will ascertain how to solve the problem and be able to solve any other problem that may appear.

Two Ways to Save

To maximize your savings potential you need to know and understand the two categories of saving:

- Saving when you earn.
- Saving when you spend.

There is no other time when you can save money.

This basic concept of putting saving into two groups also means twice as many dollars can be saved. Two different possible groups of saving give you the chance for twice as many saved dollars. You save not once, but twice! You can save when you earn money and when you spend money.

How does this system work to save twice as much? Many people believe erroneously, that you can save money only when you spend money. If the only time you could save money were when you buy something, you would hardly be able to save your way to success. It would be very difficult to save 50% of your net income this way. This is why there are two distinct times to save money. When you begin a plan of systematic savings with every paycheck, you increase your savings dramatically. When you save $.50 of every $1 you earn and add the $.50 you saved with every $1 you spent, you double your savings. That is how you save twice as much when you save when you earn *and* save when you spend.

Begin an automatic savings of 10% (or more) of every paycheck. By developing a plan in which you automatically save a portion every time you receive your paycheck, you take an important step forward in reaching success through saving. By reducing how much you have to spend (because you automatically save a percentage of every paycheck), you force yourself to live on less income. Once you are accustomed to spending less, you will be able to increase your savings from 10% to 15% or 20%. Rather than try to force yourself to spend 50% less, work toward your goal in increments. This is a crucial step in the creation of your savings program. You can reduce how much you spend and can begin saving immediately just by saving a portion of your paycheck.

Believe me—this savings method is a great money-saving technique. When you create the habit of saving a portion of every paycheck, you develop a consistency that will transmute yourself from a spender into a saver. When you begin thinking like a saver enormous benefits will begin to appear. Once you see the benefits, you will not want to stop saving. Start saving and you will continue saving.

An automatic savings of every paycheck—or, simply put, "paying yourself" out of every paycheck—is a great method for saving money. You can begin your journey to success through saving by beginning your savings immediately. How do you do that? By creating, right at this moment, an automatic savings plan. Begin right now! Stop reading (for a moment), grab your billfold, purse, or wherever you keep your money, and begin an automatic savings plan by removing 10% of whatever is in it. Even if this amounts to only a few dollars, do it anyway. Now stick your money in an enveloped marked, "savings" and put it somewhere safe. Congratulations! You are now on your way to saving your way to success!

Remove the Obstacle of Debt

There are no secrets to saving what you earn, but there are secrets about how you can make it possible. To save what you earn you need only do it, but to make it achievable, other things need to be done. In order to be able to save what is earned you must not be spending all of your income. If expenses are already taking up all of your income, then expenses first need to be reduced to be able to save. Cutting expenses can become difficult, but spending needs to be decreased in order to save money immediately as it is earned.

There are varying degrees of difficulty when trying to reduce expenses and spending. If the things you are buying are wants, not needs, than with will-power, it may be easy to change spending habits and reduce the total amount of spending dollars. If what you are buying are needs, then it becomes very difficult, because what you are buying are the necessities of life. If debt has piled up, and much of your income is going to payoff your debt, it may seem almost impossible to save any money, let alone be able to save 40 or 50%.

Debt is one of the biggest detriments that can keep you from saving. All the money you earn is going to pay mounting debts and bills and to necessary items such as food, clothing and shelter. Very little is going to wants. It would seem almost impossible to get out of this growing hole, but it can be done. A savings plan or program is meant to get you out of this rut. Debts can impede, or halt your drive to success, but they can be overcome. Debts are only obstacles waiting to be defeated.

How do you get out of debt? By taking action. Chapter twelve will discuss at length how to get out of debt—but briefly, the main keys to removing debt are resolve and strength. If you are in debt, you must stop increasing debt immediately by realizing it is an obstacle to your savings potential. This is the first step. Next, you need to invest in yourself (your greatest asset). Learn all you can. Discipline yourself to follow a savings program. Destroy all your credit cards. Set up a plan to stop paying a little on all the debts and start paying more on some debts to reduce your total debt. A plan to reduce debt to zero needs to be implemented. Debts and bills must be cut. Set "baby step" goals if necessary. Transmute yourself from spender to saver. Through resolve and strength, the cost of needs can be cut, and saving can begin.

Materialize your dreams into concrete form. Forget about the movies, or the "cool" stuff. Forget about what the neighbors think. Forget about those flashy toys or burgers the kids want. Forget the flashy clothes or the new car. Stop the status seeking and the comparison with what the neighbors have. Concentrate on the bills and debt. Remove those worries and negatives and then become a success. Take the audacious step forward. Start now. You can do it. Nothing is impossible.

Maximize Your Savings

To reach success through saving, you need to maximize your savings potential. In order to reach your maximum savings, one of the things you must do is save money almost every time you buy something. When you buy a necessity, such as food, you should be saving a percentage of the original cost, thus reducing how much you spend. When you buy something unnecessary, or wants, you should also be saving every time. Whether you are buying some clothing, or deciding what fun you want to have on Friday night, you must remember your desire to save your way to success. You need to maximize your savings, and in order to maximize your savings, one of the things you need to do is save money simultaneously when you spend money.

Like John Frugal and William Spendall, every decision you make is based on whether you are a saver or a spender. John is a saver. Even when he spends money to buy necessities, or when he, on occasion, buys some wants, he is always saving some of the original purchase price. He knows he must constantly think "save" and constantly feed his subconscious mind the thought— he is a saver. He will save all the time, and will reach success through saving. If you want to maximize your savings, you need to become a saver and begin saving all the time, even when you spend.

Saving when you spend is separated into its own two parts:

- Saving when you buy wants.
- Saving when you buy need.

Saving when you buy wants can bring out the greatest amount of saving because you do not even need to buy wants— so you save 100% when you do not buy it! The greatest technique to save the most, which is 100%, is elimination. Saving when you buy need can be much more difficult because what you are buying is necessary to live healthfully. Still, saving when you buy need can bring about rewards. To learn more on how you can save money when buying needs read on to chapter three.

Remember the basics. Save at least 10% of every paycheck. It is the beginning of your success through saving. Learn the formulas to save all the time so you can reach your maximum savings potential. Understand you can save the same dollar twice—first when you earn, then when you spend. You may be able to double your savings with this savings formula. To maximize your savings potential you also need to reduce your living expenses by saving when you buy need. If you have debt, plan to pay so much a month to creditors to begin to eliminate your debt. Implement a plan to reduce debt to zero to increase your savings potential. By investing in yourself you will be able to reduce your debt, increase your savings with the formulas of saving and reach your maximum savings potential.

Points to Ponder:

- There is almost an uncountable number of ways to save money.
- With tested proven methods, you can save as much money as you desire—as much as 50% or more of your income.
- Invest in yourself, your desires, your effort and time, your quest for knowledge, the joy of your work, your discipline, and your enthusiasm. Accustom yourself to always working toward success, and success will be yours.
- By saving continuously and forming a savings habit, you will accustom yourself to saving money. When this becomes second nature, you guarantee your success.
- To be able to save all the time you need to learn the formulas and methods for saving and to always continue to learn new formulas and methods.
- There are two basic ways to save: save when you earn and save when you spend. Using both ways will allow you to save twice as many dollars.
- Begin saving right now by starting an automatic savings plan. Take 10% of what is in your wallet or purse at this moment, put it in an envelope marked "savings" and placing it in a safe place. Congratulations! You have started down the road to success through saving!
- Debt is the one obstacle impeding a person's ability to save money. Debt can be overcome if you work hard every day to remove it.

You will not reach your savings potential until you invest in yourself to reach your savings potential.

3
SAVING WHEN YOU BUY NEEDS

*"He who understands the limits of life knows how easy
it is to procure enough to remove the pain of want and
make the whole life complete and perfect.
Hence, he has no longer any need of things which are to be
won only by labor and conflict."*

Epicurus[1]

"You can not escape necessities; but you can conquer them,"
wrote Seneca, a Roman philosopher and statesman.[2] Do not think
you cannot save on necessities, because you can. Necessities do
not have to run your life. Conquer them! Begin the savings!

Food, along with water, is the most necessary thing we need
to live. It gives us the strength and energy to grow and continue.
Some people might fear that saving on food would reduce the
quality of food they eat. The fact of the matter is we can and
should save money when buying food. As long as we still eat
healthy foods, it does not matter how much we pay for it. A
person can eat healthy and still be saving enormous amounts of
money on the food bill. People who know about saving
understand that food is an area in which some of the most
rewarding percentages of savings can take place.

The advantage of food is it has so many possibilities for how
to save when you buy it. Food has more money saving
techniques than any other necessity because it is the necessity
purchased the most frequently. Food, something we all need, is
also something we can all save on.

There are many excellent, proven methods that save money
when purchasing food. Several methods pertain specifically to
purchasing groceries, while others pertain only to eating out.
Others, including gardening, save money on all types of food
purchases because they reduce how much food needs to be

39

purchased. Some proven methods to save money when buying food are coupons, gardening and comparison shopping. Read ahead to find out how these and many other methods will save you money on your food expense.

How to Save on Groceries

The following illustration is proof you can save a substantial percentage of your grocery bill. By using the money saving techniques described in this chapter you too will be able to save 40% to 60% of your grocery bill. If your average food bill per month is $150, you would be able to save between $720 to $1,080 in a year's time.

Please examine the illustration, "Saving Money on Groceries." The total savings was $14.86 of the original price of $36.03—equaling a 41.24% savings on the total grocery bill. One key to remember is the savings are not based on the coupons alone, but it is based on the original cost before any sale or marked down price. To give you an accurate idea of the difference between the original cost and the final cost, look at the table of the groceries purchased with their original costs and final costs.

Several money saving techniques were used in this example. The most apparent and prominent was the use of vendor coupons and store coupons. Shopping at a discount grocery store also drastically reduced the final cost. Products were bought on sale and coupons reduced the price even more. The savings percentage could have been better if the Coffemate had not been purchased, but there will be some things on which you will not save money. The key to saving money on groceries is to make sure that those instances in which no money can be saved on a product are drastically reduced.

With a very good savings percentage of 40%, we had a proud shopping day. Do not expect to save enormous percentages of over 50% in every instance—the next time you may only save 20 or 25%—but do not be surprised when occasionally you are able to save as much as 50 or 60% on your grocery bill.

Saving Money on Groceries

Product	Original Cost	Final Cost
2/Coffeemate 32oz	$1.48/ea	$1.48/ea
2/Hellman 1000 Island dressing	$2.78/ea	$1.39/ea
2/Landers Cranberry juice	$2.98/ea	$1.94/ea
Baby carrots 2lbs	$2.49	$1.68
2/Ball Park Franks	$2.68/ea	$.965/ea
8/various brand pop	$.25/ea	$.15/ea
4/ 15oz cans of fruit	$.99/ea	$.65/ea
12oz bag of cookies	$1.50	$.75
8oz box of ripple chips	$1.77	$.89
12oz box of Little Debbie muffins	$1.59	$1.20
64oz of Snapple	$2.98	$1.16
Total	$36.03 (.14 tax)	$21.17(.14 tax)

COUPONS

Coupons are a big advantage to a savings minded grocery shopper. Coupons can be used anytime within their expiration dates, are readily available, and do not take as long to cut and sort as you might think. With double coupons and store coupons, big savings can be reaped. Coupons are a valuable commodity for purchasing groceries, or going out to a restaurant to eat. *The small amount of time spent cutting and sorting coupons can mean big savings of at least 25% to over 50% or 60% every time at the cashier.*

REBATES

It is even possible to earn money when saving during grocery shopping. Let us say a product is on sale at $.50 off the regular price of $1.98. A rebate form special is available for a

41

refund of $1. A coupon of $.50, that was clipped and saved, is used and gets doubled at the cashier. The final price after the double coupon is $.48. Do not forget the rebate of $1 on the product you paid $.48 for. With the rebate, you gained $.52 for buying the product! Not only was the $1.98 earned through saving when buying, but $.52 was literally earned by saving! You earned $2.50 by buying a particular product. Yes, there are people who sometimes actually earn money when they purchase something because they are canny shoppers. You can be one of them!

ON THE SHELF SAVINGS

Saving on groceries often begins even before coupons, sales and rebates. It begins on the shelf, where the savings are not as easily visible because they are not advertised sales. Always watch carefully for on the shelf savings, but make sure they are savings and not a trick. Anyone can spot a product with a big sign saying it is on sale. This person is usually the one who thinks he or she will be saving money when, in reality, the savings are not as significant as the savings a discerning, money-saving shopper will achieve. Just because it is on sale does not mean the shopper is getting the best buy. Many people clean the shelves of the sale products with the big signs, but the smart shopper spots the real bargain—perhaps the same product, but a different brand not on sale, for which a coupon decreases the price below the price of the "big" sales item. The store may be making more money on the sale item because it distracts customers from the cheaper brand with the regular price. Always make sure the savings are actually there and the store is not just trying to get you to buy a particular name brand.

GENERIC BRANDS

Buying generic brands is a good money-saving technique, but not always. Generics may have a lower price, but what happens when the more expensive product goes on sale or you have a coupon? With a sale or coupon, the more expensive product may become cheaper than the store brand. The resourceful shopper will be vigorous in spotting the best bargain during any particular shopping experience, and not habitually buy what was the best bargain the last time. One week it may be wise to buy product A, but the next week it could be product B that is cheaper. The smart shopper watches and checks everything.

FUTURE BUYING

The resourceful shopper will also use the technique of future buying. Future buying is when a shopper, because of the enormous bargain, will buy extra to have on hand for the future. If there is a spectacular buy, smart shoppers will buy it, if they know it will be needed in the future (and the product will not spoil by the time it is used). As long as the product will be used, it is worth purchasing items you will not need for a while. This technique will not work for perishable refrigerated items, but it will work for any shelf items, or anything that can be frozen, such as margarine, butter and meats. Never overbuy, so items no longer fit in the available freezer space, or items have to be thrown out due to spoilage. As long as you can remember what is in the cupboards and freezer, rotate items, and rarely throw anything out because of spoiling or lack of space, then future buying will save money.

BUYING BULK

Buying bulk is another on-the-shelf saving technique. The small, 16-oz. box costs an expensive $2; two equal to 32 oz., would cost $4. The big 32-oz. box only costs $3.50—a savings of $.50. Although this is a rather simple example it clearly shows the savings possibilities of buying in bulk.

Once again, every instance needs a new evaluation. If only 24 oz. of the big 32-oz. box can be used before it rots, than $.50 has been lost. In the small box, 24 oz. costs only $3. And it would be better to buy the small box if a sale, or a coupon brings the small box under the price of $1.75; then it becomes cheaper than the big box. Every instance has different possibilities for saving.

MARKED-DOWN PRODUCTS

Marked-down products are another method to save on groceries. Some people believe if a package is not perfect the product inside is not fit to eat. As long as the food is still safe, there is nothing wrong with buying mark-down food. If food products were unhealthy, the stores would not be selling them. Try a bread store to buy bread at much cheaper prices. You can find day-old whole wheat bread loaves at the price of 2 for $1.69, while at the supermarket you are forced to purchase the "cheapest" brand at $1.69 per loaf. By shopping at the bread store, you saved $.85 per loaf. Shop at discount stores for brand name foods (that may or may not have rips or dings or dents in the packaging) at cheaper prices compared to the big grocery stores. Buying mark-downs, a mostly overlooked money saving technique, can be used whenever it is the cheaper price, to save money.

There are many other methods of saving when grocery shopping:

- Shopping when you are not hungry in order to prevent impulse buying.
- Make a list and stick to it.
- Use the store's box or tote bag if they give you a small credit for using it rather than plastic bags.
- Shop regularly rather than only once every few weeks so you can spot specials.
- Stock up cupboards and home freezers when awesome, super-saving buys come along.
- Plan ahead for what you will need within the next few weeks so you will have a chance to watch for the products when they come on sale.

Avoid buying at the convenience store. Plan ahead to always be prepared so milk and bread will not have to be bought at the

44

more expensive convenience store. Convenience has become an enormous part of our everyday lives, compared to only a few decades ago. The extra cost on the price tag is what you are paying for the convenience. With only a small amount of planning of what food you will need, you will be able to stay away from the high-priced convenience stores and save yourself money.

Grocery shopping can be expensive. To the smart shopper who wants to save, grocery shopping is not expensive, but is a time to save a lot of money. One week may bring in only a savings of 20%, but the next week can bring in a whopping 50% savings. With every shopping experience, there is a different challenge.

Do not get discouraged. You may run into a few shopping times when the savings are low, especially when you first start smart-shopping. As you understand how to maximize to the fullest your savings by mixing and matching several methods, as you begin to learn the normal prices of products and what is a good buy, your savings will grow. Change your old spending habits into more productive and gratifying saving habits. Watch your savings increase dramatically as you continue to gain knowledge and experience in smart grocery shopping.

John Frugal and William Spendall

Our two friends, John Frugal and William Spendall, have inadvertently met at the grocery store. Each is out purchasing groceries for the next two weeks. Some items included on each shopping list include hamburger, milk, cereal, tissue paper, soup, flour, bread, rice, vegetables, and snack chips.

Our two friends meet outside the store to compare their receipts to see how much was spent, saved, and what percentage was saved. After shopping, William is almost certain he will beat John in savings. The comparison begins with a look at what groceries were purchased. Relatively the same types of food were purchased, except John had some generic brands and some mark-down products. William blurted out he had saved over $5 on his grocery bill, but after examination of John's receipt, William knew who had saved the most.

William had gone to the grocery store unprepared and hungry. He ended up searching through his unorganized coupon box for coupons while in the store, to only get frustrated and buy the first item he saw. He also bought with his stomach and not with his head. John, on the other hand, had prepared by searching through grocery ads, categorizing his coupons, and planned ahead. John used more than just the coupon method. He also used the methods of comparison shopping, planning, buying bulk, buying markdowns, and any and every other method he could use. John mixed and matched the methods of saving on groceries to save nearly $20—four times as much as William, and 35% of John's total bill. John Frugal was a prudent, canny shopper; William Spendall was not.

Eating Out Less = Huge Savings

Grocery shopping is not the only way to save money on food. Eating out is another time when a person can save money. If you ate out one less time a week or even a month, consider how much money you could save. What if you did not eat out at all? Lots of money could be earned through saving. Think back to the last time you ate out. How much did it cost you? How could your money been put to better use? Eating out occasionally is a nice way to relax, or celebrate. Eating out frequently is a money drain, and a detriment to saving money and reaching success.

Restaurants are making a lot of money from today's fast-paced America. It's estimated that U.S. Consumers will spend $399.2 billion eating out[3]—a staggering amount of money being spent on prepared foods. Rather than becoming a part of this statistic, cook and eat at home.

Americans spend far too much money and time at the restaurants. In 1970, 34% of food dollars were spent away from home. In 1995, 46% of food dollars were spent away from home.[4] Almost half of all money spent on food is going to the restaurants, candy machines, etc. Rather than throwing away your money, use it to buy groceries, which would save you a tremendous amount of money. Rather than eat out all of the time and spending your money, eat out only occasionally and save your money.

Do not eat out because you "need" to, but because you "want" to. Many people complain of being too busy to make meals; therefore, the family "needs" to eat out all the time. When was the last time you went out to eat to celebrate, or relax, rather than because you were in a hurry, did not have the time to cook, did not want to cook, did not have food at home to cook, or did not want to clean dirty dishes? Stop eating out because you "have" to and you will start saving money.

After cutting back how many instances you eat out, you can also save more money each time you do eat out—all you need to do is use coupons and be aware of specials. If you can buy a restaurant coupon book for ten dollars, use only a few coupons and save over ten dollars, it is worth it. Save the coupons in newspapers, then use some occasionally to save money, then it is worth the minute time to grab and collect those coupons. Rather than go to the more expensive restaurant, go to the restaurant running a special or use a coupon. Yes, every time you eat out, you can save.

Reduce Intake of Fats, Oils, and Sweets to Save Money and Your Health

One particular food bill some people overlook when trying to save money is snacks and pop. Candy bars, pop, chips and ice cream have become a part of everyday eating, yet many times they are overlooked when saving money on food because they are normally bought on the run. To save money and health, reduce how much candy and junk food you buy. Fats, oils and sweets (in your candy bar and can of pop) are, according to the USDA's Food Guide Pyramid, to be eaten sparingly, so by moderating how much of these you eat you not only save money, but your health as well. By reducing the amount of candy you eat, you will save your teeth. By eating less calories and fat, you may begin to lose weight (with also an exercise program being performed). By eating healthier foods, you will lead a healthier life. By reducing the amount of junk food, you will reap many benefits.

And of course, there are financial benefits to consider. Snacks and pop are expensive, especially when you do not buy them at the grocery store. The prices are greatly inflated in those candy and pop machines, at the game or concert, or at the gas station. The simplest and most effective way to save money on snacks and pop is to cut them out completely. Since everyone likes a candy bar every once and a while, rather than trying to eliminate all pop and snacks, you just need to use your savvy to save money on these items. How do you do that? Stop buying the marked-up foods in the vending machines, at convenience stores and at events. Buy everything cheaper at the grocery store, and then pack it in your lunch for work, or when you go on a trip. You will quickly reduce how much you are spending.

Self-discipline should also be used to create the maximum savings. You will not improve your health unless you moderate, or reduce, how much junk food you are buying. You will not be maximizing your savings unless you reduce how much you are buying. This is the most effective way to save on snacks and pop. The savings are enormous when junk food and pop are used with moderation.

Gardening

One particular key when trying to save money on your food bill is to grow an organic garden whenever possible. By planting a garden you will enjoy eating fresh produce—squash, carrots, lettuce, cantaloupe, radishes, onions, potatoes—and save enormous amounts of money. Certainly some time will go into a garden, but compared to the savings it will procure, the amount of time spent gardening will be well worth the effort.

One of the best ways to save money on your food bill is with an organic garden. You can save hundreds, maybe thousands of dollars from a few dollars worth of seeds and a little time and effort. It does take some time, but the food from the garden is almost free. Once you become a good gardener, you could even start selling your produce to actually earn money from your garden. Organic gardening is a very effective method to save money.

When you grow your own produce, you eliminate many expenses you are paying at the grocery store for fruits and vegetables. When you buy produce at the store, only a small amount of the price is actually going to buying the food. You are paying for the shipping and handling. You are paying for the expense and time of growing. You are also paying the grocery store for storing and keeping it fresh. When you grow your own organic garden you eliminate all of that. The only costs you have are a few dollars for some seeds and maybe a first-time expense of some gardening tools and equipment. By growing your own organic garden, you will reap huge amounts of saving while enjoying delicious, fresh produce.

When you garden, can and freeze also. By canning and freezing, you continue reaping garden savings far into the winter when the garden is covered under a blanket of snow. Canning and freezing is not hard, and although it may take some time to learn and then to do successfully, it takes little money.

Do you want to enjoy fresh produce all year long? Do you desire to save money from your gardening efforts all year long? Of course you do. In order to do that, though, you need to can and freeze. It may take some time, especially when it is your first time, but consider the possibility you will be able to enjoy your gardening efforts all year long and you will be willing to use some time to can and freeze.

Everyone should have a garden, whether it be a full acre for someone on a farm or just a few tomato plants and some carrots and lettuce in the back yard or on the patio. No matter what size, a garden can save money. If you live in town, take the time to search for areas in and/or around town to grow a garden. Many cities contain gardening areas within city limits where numerous residents grow their own garden patch.

However, gardens are overlooked or refused as a method to save money because they require work. Do not look at the work;

look at the savings instead. With even a small garden you will save money.

Stop Throwing Out Money as Food

Another big money-saving technique is reducing how much you throw out. Stop wasting food. There are hungry people out there who would be glad to have it.

Wasted food equals wasted money. If you throw out a moldy loaf of bread, you wasted the $1.50 you paid for the bread. If the bread had been eaten before it spoiled, the $1.50 would have gone to good use. Stop wasting food and start saving money.

John Frugal and William Spendall

William Spendall is thirsty. He pours himself a glass full of orange juice. Several hours go by, and he forgets about it, having only drunk half of the full glass. William decides he was not as thirsty as he first assumed and will leave the glass of juice in the refrigerator for later. When William returns home from the store, he pours himself another glass, forgetting about the one he placed in the refrigerator earlier in the day (now shuffled to the back of the refrigerator). Before he can drink the second glass, William leaves again unexpectedly, forgetting it on the table. Dinner comes. William comes home, and sits down and prepares to eat. He notices someone left a half drank glass of orange juice on the table. By now it is all warm, and no one will drink it. William dumps it down the sink. He pours himself another full glass of juice for dinner, but again only drinks half of it. During the evening after supper he pours himself another glass, but this time pours it only half full. He is not thirsty and does not want to waste orange juice. He drinks the full amount of the half-filled glass, but he has forgotten about all the other half-filled glasses he has left around the house. William has also forgotten about the one he specifically put in the refrigerator so he would drink it later and not waste it. By the time bedtime comes, the thirsty

William Spendall may have several half-full glasses sitting around the house. William has wasted juice and money without even realizing it. With no discipline and desire—as shown by his waste of juice—William will not become a success as quickly as John Frugal will.

Do you find yourself wasting food? Is there always a small pile of food on your plate when you are done eating? Do you sometimes order a big meal at a restaurant and then do not eat all of it? Do you sometimes take something, but because you decide you do not like it, waste it? Stop being like Williams Spendall. Stop "garbaging" your money as discarded food and start moving toward success.

Many people, especially children, never learn to finish what is on their plates. A little while after supper, they are hungry again, while the good food on their supper plate was dumped. According to Helen Palit, director of City Harvest, a charitable organization in New York City that picks up food leftovers and takes them to soup kitchens and homeless shelters, approximately 20% of the food in the United States is wasted.[5] Americans throw out way too much food—the same as throwing out money. When was the last time you noticed yourself not eating everything on your plate? You are wasting money. Even worse is when you order from a restaurant, and do not eat the food, which is ultimately thrown out. Not only is food wasted, but it is expensive, prepared food. Significant amounts of money are wasted if this is a habit.

Stop "garbaging" your money. Throwing out food is the same as throwing out money. You did pay for the food did you not? You paid money for the unused portion of food being "garbaged." You are "garbaging" your money that went to buy the food being wasted. Do not throw out your hard earned money and pretend you are throwing out garbage. Is *your* money garbage?

Teach your kids (and maybe yourself) good food and money savings habits. One bad habit kids have all too often is to open a full can of pop, drink a quarter or half of it, then let the rest go to waste. A little bit later they do the same thing, and yet adults wonder why they are always thirsty. These children must have learned from William Spendall's habits. Teach your whole family how to not waste food and save money in the process.

Save Money When Buying Clothing

It is possible and easy to save money on clothing. Although there are not many coupons for clothing, the savings are still possible. The best method to save on clothing is simply not to constantly buy new clothes, or at least not buy them very often. Moderation and other techniques will save you money when buying clothing.

Rummage sales, garage sales and thrift stores are all gateways to saving money on clothes. These bargain hunter stores will save you a significant amount of money. Secondhand stores can help you save money on many things, but clothes are one of the biggest items. If you are a conscientious shopper, you will be able to find nearly new, excellent clothes for reasonable prices at these secondhand places. Some people abhor even the suggestion of purchasing secondhand clothes. As long as care is taken to completely wash the clothing before using, and as long as the clothing is still in nearly new shape, why not? You will still look "stylish," and will also be a savvy shopper at the same time. You should not feel embarrassed by shopping at these places, but should feel intelligent and savvy because of all the money you will save.

There are other methods that will help you save money on your clothing expenditure. Buy only when there is a sale. Shop around at different stores. Do not purchase spontaneously, but wait, and purchase smartly by buying when the clothes are on sale. Do not buy the latest fashion when it comes out, buy a new outfit for every new occasion coming up, or buy because you just want to have something new. And forget the name brands. Why pay double, triple or even higher prices just for the name of the product? When you have the choice of the same two items in quality and performance, why pay more for the one that has the "name" brand? You can not save as much through these techniques as through second-hand buying, but they will still save you money.

Reduce the amount of clothes you buy to save money. Stop filling up the closet with new outfits. Start wearing what you already have. Stop buying the new fad all the time; instead, buy something that will look nice for a long time and take care of it. A person should not need all the clothes they many times have. Those lifeless clothes dangling in the closet collecting dust cost you well earned money. Not to use them is a waste of money.

Try to reduce the amount of clothing you have to buy with other techniques. You might learn how to sew. Mend the rip or lost button rather than tossing the shirt or pants. With the kids, use hand-me downs. Try not to destroy your good clothes. Wear work clothes whenever you think there is a good probability something might happen to your clothes as you work or do other things that might damage the clothes. Have a pair of work clothes on hand to use so it will not hurt if they get a hole, dirty, or greased up. If you reduce the amount you buy, you are saving.

Do not forget to have your own garage sale to sell those outdated or outgrown clothes. If they are still in reasonable shape other people can probably use them. A person should sell on a rummage sale the clothes not used to earn money to buy the clothes needed.

You Can Save Money on All Necessities

You can save money on other necessities as well. Save on electricity by using florescent light bulbs; they last ten times longer, and usually cost less than ten times as much. Save on heat at night during the winter by using an extra blanket and turning down the thermostat. Open the drapes and let the sunshine in during the winter to warm the home and save on heating costs. Do the opposite in the summer by closing the drapes to keep the hot sun out, and opening the windows to let the cool breeze blow through.

Save by buying used rather than new. Instead of buying a $250 tool set, half of which you will not even use, complete the partial set you may already have by shopping at tool discount stores, pawn shops and rummage sales. Cut down on necessary expenses by learning how to and doing it yourself. This is a great money saving technique. You can use it again and again with no more high repair and maintenance bills. There are always possibilities to save. Use your imagination to create new ways to save on necessities.

Possibly the simplest, and most effective money-saving method for necessities is to buy used. Every necessity, except food, you can buy used. You can shop at second hand stores, rummage sales and garage sales and find perfectly good items at a fraction of the cost an identical item would cost new. You can buy clothes, furniture, dishes, appliances, tools and equipment all at a fraction of the cost, just because the items have been used. As long as they are usable there is nothing wrong with buying items used. You may be thinking you saved a lot of money by buying new furniture on sale, but the savings pales in comparison to when you buy used, good quality furniture. If you are not buying used, you should be.

One particular necessity, transportation (especially your own car or vehicle) can be very expensive. Carpool when the opportunity is available to save on your automobile fuel bill, or use the bus, or better yet walk. Some times, though, it is very impractical to reduce automobile use. There are far too many times when you must have your own transportation, such as for business. The second best method is to do maintenance and small repairs yourself. Learning how to do repairs on anything is a great money-saving method (learn more about this in chapter nine). It is especially great given the expensive cost of automobile repairs. You can save money on your transportation cost if you reduce your use and learn how to do small repairs and maintenance on your automobile.

There are all kinds of opportunities to save money on necessities. Go to a barber college, rather than a salon or barber. The price may be half the price you would normally pay. This could also work for dental schools, and other schools or colleges that have services in your area.

Even by taking care of your health, you save money in several ways. You decrease health-related bills including doctor bills and medications. You increase your efficiency, allowing better use of your time to earn and save more. You also reduce lost time and lost income from sick days. Synchronize money saving with good health by exercising, by walking rather than driving sometimes, and by reducing the intake of junk food. Take action to change your habits to create good health, and your savings will increase simultaneously.

A home can be the most expensive necessity of all. To save the most, purchase in full. Impossible? Absolutely not! If you follow the concepts in this book, you may, after becoming successful, be able to purchase a house in full and save an enormous amount of money in interest.

What do you do before then? One option is to purchase a trailer house. It costs much less than a house, and rather than renting, where the money is spent, you still have your money. Like a house, the trailer home is an asset. Purchase it in full, and when it is time to move, you will be able to sell it and get some of your money back—or maybe even all of it and more, if you made improvements.

When you are in the market to buy a house you must be patient. There are ways to save money, but you must remember—your house is not an expense, it is an investment. If you can, save money by buying when interest rates are low, or by finding a motivated seller. Never jump into an agreement as big as buying a house, though, just to save a little money. Buying a house is a major investment, you must be patient, and buy only when you have found the house you and your family will enjoy for many years.

If apartment living is your option, you can save money by becoming the manager or caretaker of a building sized so you can handle the extra work above your regular job. This is a great (and often missed) money-saving idea. Rent is expensive, but if you use this proven method you will save money to reach success while living in an apartment.

How I Did It

Back in chapter two when I described how I was able to easily reach a saving rate of over 50%, I saved some money on my automobile gas expenditure by walking to a barber college. By going to the barber college rather than a regular hair stylist or barber, I was able to save approximately 50% on each haircut, which cost me only $5 per haircut! I also walked to other businesses located within a short fifteen- or twenty-minute walk. By walking to the barber college (and gas) and spending less for my haircuts.

How do I save on transportation? I operate two vehicles, one for work, and one for good; therefore, only one gets enormous amounts of wear and tear, while the other stays in near mint shape.

When I described back in chapter two how I was able to save over 50% of my income, one method I used to increase my income through secondary incomes was apartment managing and care taking. I waited patiently for an opportunity for a caretaker or manager position to become available. When a caretaker position in a building I like did become available, I grabbed it. You must do the same. You need to begin your search to find a secondary income in apartment building caretaking or managing.

A key to saving, especially in saving when you spend to buy need, is to weigh the cost versus the savings. If the cost is higher then the savings, then there are no savings at all. A simple example is a product that lasts only twice as long, but costs more than twice as much. The savings are not there. Watch sales and promotions, and prudently buy the product that will last the longest *and* save the most at the same time.

Let us say you need a new furnace. One furnace on the market is the geo-thermal heat pump. There are no fuel or gas bills, because it takes heat from the ground to heat your home. By purchasing the geo-thermal heating system, a person pays more money when initially purchased and installed, and does not save immediately, but with the savings that incur after several years, the money saved by reducing heating costs means the geo-thermal system will easily surpass the savings of other furnaces and will quickly pay for itself. Always compute and verify what the savings will be in the long run, not just when you purchase an item. Use moderation and cost versus savings to save when buying needs.

Luxuries of Yesterday Are not Necessities of Today

Stop turning the luxuries of yesterday into the necessities of today. When your net worth becomes more, it does not mean you need more things and have to spend more and buy expensive, luxury items. You only need the basics. Anything beyond that is things you want. Stop turning those luxuries, items that were not affordable when you did not have the money to afford them, into needs just because you now have the money to buy them. Needs are always needs and wants are always wants, no matter how wealthy or poor you may be.

It is easy to procure and establish what is necessary to live. Many people actually buy too much need. The extra product then becomes only wants when they actually consider it necessary. The rest of the "need" over what is actually needed is actually only wants or "adult toys." "Most people simply don't understand that they cannot have both money and things—at least, in the beginning! To accumulate money, you must give up things. But if you accumulate things, you will never have money. It is just that simple, and yet few people really understand it," wrote Glen Bland.[6] Stop turning the luxuries of yesterday into the necessities of today and you will save a significant amount of money. And the reward can be much sweeter because of the effort you put into saving that money. You can save on buying needs. Anyone can do it. You can do it. Begin now!

Points to Ponder:

- Mix and match the multitude of methods of saving when buying groceries: coupons, planning, comparison shopping, buying mark-downs, shopping discount stores. Save money every time you shop for groceries.
- Eat out only on special occasions, not when you "need" to because you do not want to cook, or all the dishes are dirty or some other excuse. Reduce how many times you eat out and the money you spend.
- To save money and your health, reduce your use of fats, oils, and sweets including the candy bar and can of pop out of the vending machine.
- Grow and preserve your own organic garden produce.
- Wasted food equals wasted money. Whenever food is thrown out in your home, the money that bought the food is being thrown out.
- Shop for clothes at clean secondhand stores to reduce the amount you spend on clothing.
- Use moderation, weigh the cost versus the savings, and comparison shop when buying necessities to save money on all necessities.
- Shop at rummage sales, garage sales, and second-hand stores.
- When shopping for a home remember—it is an investment, not an expense, be patient, and choose wisely, rather than on impulse.
- Stop buying things you think are necessities but are only wants, "things", or "adult toys", and start saving money toward your success.

**Stop turning the luxuries of yesterday
into the necessities of today.**

4
SAVING WHEN YOU BUY WANTS

*"It is the preoccupation with possession,
more than anything else,
that prevents man from living freely and nobly."*

Bertrand Russell[1]

There is no better process for saving money than moderation when you buy wants, or things. By not buying something, you save 100%! There is no other method that can be proven to do that every time! To save big when you buy wants you only have to cut back on how much you buy. It is that simple! Use moderation and elimination and you will increase your savings dramatically.

Many people do not realize they can save 100% by not buying an item. You could save 100% all the time just by not buying any wants. It is possible, but not very feasible. It would mean eliminating everything you want. Who would want to do that? Instead, you can still dramatically increase your savings by reducing your purchases of things you do not *need*. Reduce how much you are spending, and watch how your savings grow.

Individual Thinkers Do Not Follow the Crowd

Some people consider erroneously, that they are big money savers when they buy name brand-clothes on sale, or rent movies instead of going to the expensive theater, or use a coupon when they eat out. This is far from the truth. Sure, they are saving, but it is insignificant compared to how much they would save if they would eliminate, or reduce, those expenditures. Rather than save some money by using a coupon or other method, by simply not buying, you would save 100%. The twenty dollars that would have gone to buy something will now be in the bank earning interest. Eliminate one movie, or one dinner out, and save 100% for that instance. You can save when you buy wants by using saving techniques like coupons or comparison shopping, but to save a sizable amount of money, when you buy wants, you should eliminate some of the unneeded things you are buying.

How much would you rather save—the full twenty dollars and 100%, with the money-saving method, moderation and elimination, or a meager 20%, or four dollars, with a coupon? The more you save the more expeditiously success will be reached. The more you save, the surer guarantee of success through saving.

You can save substantial amounts of money by eliminating, or reducing some of the unneeded things you buy. Cut down on your expenses. Go without one movie, or the name brand purchased just because it is what is "cool." Reduce how much want you buy by half, and you automatically are saving 50%. It is easy and simple. Use your will-power to give something up, by half, and immediately begin saving 50%.

Do not become a part of the crowd who spends their way to sorrow; rather become one of the few who saves to success. Do not save money to pay for the status symbol or luxury item as some other people do to be part of the crowd. Become a leader in your community, not a person who spends money to compete with the neighbors. After you have reached success, you can continue forward and acquire riches, easily surpassing the others who did not save for success. Become an individual thinker, not a passive watcher. Become a person who desires and will reach success. Become independent, self-reliant, and happy. Thomas Edison said: "Five percent of the people think; ten percent of the people think they think; and the other eighty-five percent would rather die than think." Become one of the few who thinks. Become one of the few who is successful in life. *Become a doer of things rather than a buyer of things.*

Saving when you buy wants can bring about the most and easiest savings. For example, say you spend $100 per month for movies (theaters and rentals), but you reduce your movie allowance by 50%. You automatically save $50! With the remaining $50 allowance, you use other money saving techniques to reduce it by 50%, or $25. Your total savings become $75 or 75%! It is awesome!

Sometimes people only think of reducing how much they pay for the wants, and do not consider eliminating the wants. These people only enjoy 25% savings. The person who reduces how many wants are purchased, then saves on the remaining wants purchased, is the person who is saving 75%.

There simply is no other method out there that can save so much money and yet be so easy to use. What you need to do to use this method is simply live below your income. One could do as John Lubbock, an English scientist and banker, said: "Before buying anything, it is wise to ask if one could do without it." Ask yourself this question every time and you will, even if slowly at first, reduce how many possessions, or wants, you buy. Start living below your means, and start saving your way to success

Some people do not understand the concept of reducing how much they buy. They save when buying wants by buying on sale, buying cheaper or using coupons, but they have never even considered reducing how much they buy. Stop saving a little and start saving a lot. Begin saving a plethora of money by using the method of elimination and moderation to reduce how many things are purchased. Rather than saving a trivial sum when you buy those new curtains and rugs, because the neighbors just did, save an abundance by simply not buying them. Do not save 25% when buying the curtains, but save 100% by not buying them at all. Use moderation and elimination when you buy wants and you will increase your savings many times over.

Raise Your Standards for Saving

Maybe you have considered spending less then you earn; but, you dislike the idea of not having as many things as the neighbors. Will it really lower your standards? Actually, it depends on what you consider standards. Is a standard keeping up with the neighbors? Is a standard eating the $20 steak or fish compared to the $10 steak or fish? Depending on what you consider standards, saving could lower your standards. If designer jeans, expensive restaurants, and wasting money are standards, of course these standards will be lowered. But saving will not lower the standard of a healthy life, good food on the table, or even respectable clothing, nor will it lower the standard of reaching success, and the riches that can follow. The short time of deprivation of wants will easily be recompensed in the joys of success and riches it will procure. Realize early on in life that following the crowd and keeping up with the Joneses is not a standard; instead, having money and becoming a success should be your standard.

In order for saving to be the key for success, you must reduce or eliminate status-seeking efforts and expenditures. Status seekers are not successful. They only think they are because they have many things, which more often than not have a string of debt attached. Certainly people can seek status after becoming successful, but status seekers will never reach success because they are constantly spending beyond their means. Vance Packard wrote: "As you go up the class scale, you find people tend to develop, as a status right, a more delaying attitude toward monthly bills. A semi-upper-class wife is likely to consider it 'plebeian' to pay bills promptly and expects trades people to maintain a patient, hat-in-hand attitude. The man and wife are much too busy with larger matters to bother with bills. *Actually, of course, they are often strapped.*" (emphasis added).[3]

Do you reckon saving would be a hindrance to your status or standards? Do you fear you would no longer be able to buy all those fancy items or go to all those social events if you started saving? Too many times, society creates the impression a person must buy, buy and buy more in order to maintain status and keep up with the neighbors. Shopping has become a ritual where purchases made are not *needed*, but are purchased only to reconfirm prestige and status. When you maximize your savings you give up prestige and status symbols—but *what is more important? The status of debt, or the sweetness of success?*

Why not sacrifice some now to have tenfold in the future? Spend less now so you will have more in your future. If you become a saver, you will quickly surpass the neighborhood spenders, who will always continue to spend all they earn and live paycheck to paycheck. Think of it as sacrificing a few things when you are young so you will have a lot when you are older. Most people want to become rich, but they do not want to sacrifice now to become rich in the future. Wait for the new television, do not buy the new car, reduce how much is spent, save your money, and watch eagerly as success becomes achievable. Your sacrifice now will recompense you in the future.

Live below your means now to have a large nest egg in your future. By taking action, you will reach success. For example, when you are young, put your wants on a diet so you will remain debt-free and have a bundle of money a few years down the road. To have $10,000 to $25,000 in an investment account and a savings account by the time you are 21 years old not only provides you with a grand sense of security, it is your rocket-booster for success. Read this last statement again and think about what it could do for you.

Self-discipline Is Requisite to Saving Your Way to Success

If you desire to save your way to success, you need to discipline yourself (one of the ingredients to investing in yourself in chapter two) to reduce how many wants you are buying. This action should occur at the same time that you begin to convert from a spender into a saver. When you desire to save and discipline yourself to form habits around your desire, you will be well on your way to saving your way to success.

Use you will-power to resist buying the candy bar. Refuse to go out to eat because you "feel like it." Take heart and succeed. You can reduce your expenditures. You can increase how much you save. Courage and will-power will lead you through the difficult task to the fruits of your labor. It is possible. Whatever you desire to succeed at, you can do it.

With any goal there are obstacles. Nothing worth achieving is accomplished with ease. Everyone has obstacles to overcome, for everyone has different dreams and goals to accomplish, and every obstacle means something different to every person. Obstacles are meant to slow momentum and impede travels, but not to stop movement. People who let obstacles stop them will not be the people who will acquire success. You, on the other hand, will not let obstacles stop you for long. You will discipline yourself to use your strengths and abilities to devise a means of overcoming each obstacle. Do you have the discipline to over come your obstacles? You are the type of person who will succeed!

Spending Can Become an Addiction

Do you consider shopping a hobby? If yes, then you have become addicted to spending money. Like alcohol, drugs, smoking, gambling, or anything else done or used continuously in a harmful manner, spending can also become an addiction, and when it does, it becomes very difficult to conquer. Spending becomes an addiction when it cannot be stopped. When spending cannot be stopped, it is more aptly named "compulsive spending."

Compulsive spending can be a hard obstacle to remove. When spending has become an addiction, outside forces may be necessary to help remove the obstacle named compulsive spending. The best solution is to never become addicted. The alternatives are slim. Bankruptcy is the end result of compulsive spending. After bankruptcy, the healing begins, with restructuring, financial help, debt removal and so forth. Before bankruptcy, the addiction just continues to eat away. Maybe reading *Saving Your Way to Success* will give you the medicine and the power to get out of this strangling addiction. Compulsive spending, the start of the road to bankruptcy, is a big obstacle which must be conquered.

When you come home from the grocery store with a lot more than you had planned, you have shopped compulsively. Compulsive spending comes from lack of discipline. You see it, and you buy it; but, if you had not seen it, you would not have bought it. You may run across super deals once and awhile that will save you money on a product you did not plan to buy at a particular time, but will use in the future. Buying these is normal and is a part of the master plan of saving. When unanticipated spending happens consistently, develops into a burden, and turns into the purchase of products that you have no plausible reason to purchase, it becomes a problem: an addiction to spending, compulsive spending.

Compulsive spending can lead to catastrophe—debt, bankruptcy, and financial failure—unless you take the steps immediately and throughout your life to reduce the risk of this occurring! Stop it where it starts. Start living below your means. Start spending less. Start truly desiring success. Using moderation when spending and investing in yourself, together, is the cure compulsive spending. Reduce how much you spend and reduce your chances of transmuting into a "compulsive spender." Desire with all your heart, mind, soul, and body to rid yourself of this "disease."

Stop Loaning, or Giving, Your Money Away

Compulsive spending is the biggest obstacle, but there is another obstacle to saving that is just as important to introduce and explain—free money. This is exactly what is being produced when you lend out a dollar here, a few dollars there, to friends and never get it back. It becomes free money to your friends. The same is true, if you are always buying your friends a drink, lunch or whatever, whenever your friends say they are short on cash. When this becomes a constant and a never-returned favor, it becomes free money. Giving out free money is another obstacle that must be completely removed. Free money is money being spent; therefore, it is money which is not saved towards success.

Eliminate the obstacle of giving out free money to clear a path on the road to success.

Moochers, as they are sometimes called, are blocking your way to savings and success. These moochers are taking your money and using you. They are like parasites living freely off of a host. They get what they want and need, while you, the host, do all the work to make sure of their survival. Cut off these parasites (users and abusers) from the host (you and your money) so you can start saving.

John Frugal and William Spendall

Let us turn again to our two paradoxical friends. William Spendall has a friend who has become an obstacle in William's quest for riches. The friends have a good relationship, and have been friends for several years. Neither has much money and so together, they are always coming up with new, sometimes odd ideas to make money. Most ideas falter out of commission, but the two friends always keep trying. They, especially William Spendall, know not to try means failure, but as long as they keep trying, one day success will be theirs.

William is the host. Unbeknownst to him, he has been spending more money than his friend, Beggar Bob, because Beggar Bob has been using him. A deal is set up where they each get half of the profits, but the expenses are not split the same. William always pays more. Bob knows this, but does not care, because he is the parasite. He wants to become rich and successful, but wants William to take him there on a free ride. This type of person will never reach success without the help of someone else.

The problem is William will probably never reach success either, as long as he has this obstacle, Beggar Bob. Whenever they do something, Bob is always short of money, so William has to pay. It happens all the time. William picks up the tab or bill this time and that time, but it never seems to be Bob's turn. This is how a one-way relationship works. John Frugal, William's true friend tries to warn William about what is happening, but William shrugs it off as rubbish. After all, Beggar

Bob is his close friend. William will never get ahead, because Beggar Bob is thieving all of William's effort, money and chance for success. This is a classic example of how a parasite, Beggar Bob, gets free money from the host, William Spendall, while simultaneously dragging the host down.

Parasites never do any good, especially when *you* are the host and you are trying to get ahead in life. These rapacious parasites, the moochers, never devour enough. They will always want more and more. Even when success and riches are achieved, the parasites will still feed off the host. It is up to you to turn them away so at least you can achieve success. Refuse to give them money. If they will not change, stop trying to change them and move on with your life. At least you can reach your goals by sawing off these shackles. Emancipate yourself from the moochers.

Loaning out money, except in a formal matter, is also included in the free money obstacle, because it is very closely interrelated with the giving out of money to moochers. When a formal, written agreement is signed between the two parties, loans between family and friends are fine. There are many excellent reasons why a loan not from a institution can be very beneficial for both parties. If there is no signed agreement, though, the loan is the same as free money.

Whether the person is your own parent, sibling, or best friend, when the time comes to getting back the money, it simply will not be there much of the time if there is not a signed agreement. Why? Because the borrower is family or friend, and probably thinks the money is free and that you will not do much of anything except argue to get it back! The borrower may also think since it came from family it was a gift, not a loan—or that there are no terms, including interest, or that there is an unlimited time to pay off the loan. Whether you said differently does not matter, because when the borrower refutes what you said, it will be one person's word against another. Without a written agreement, a loan between family and friends will culminate in the loan probably ending up not being paid.

Sometimes a person does need to borrow money, and lending to family and friends when done with a written agreement, does work and can be very beneficial. But remember, an informal, verbal agreement will not stand up in court. The borrower looking for these types of loans is the type of borrower who probably will not even consider repaying the loan, ever! Excuses will be made, more time will be given, but in the end the money probably will not be returned. It becomes free money.

In order to become successful, you must eliminate this obstacle. You cannot have moochers who live off you. You cannot be loaning out money informally, or under a verbal agreement; you probably will not get it back. You are giving away money that was supposed to be accumulated to reach success.

Disorganization Costs Money

Have you ever had to purchase an item on a trip because you forgot yours at home? Have you ever misplaced a tool, then had to go and buy another one when you needed it? Are you prone to losing your keys? Do you spend a substantial amount of time looking for things you have misplaced? These are all signs of disorganization.

When you are disorganized, you are wasting precious time and effort. When you have to waste time looking for a missing set of keys, rather than using the time constructively, you lose the time forever. Time is money, so when disorganization takes up a substantial amount of your time, disorganization is costing you money. A disorganized person, for example, will waste countless hours searching through a filing cabinet for a specific paper. One of his excuses may be, "I do not have the time right now to organize my files." Yet this person would rather waste more time searching for files than schedule a time during his day to organize those files. Take the time to organize your files, your living quarters, and your life, to save time and money.

The next time you are forced to buy something you used to have, but lost or misplaced, ask yourself how much of a detriment to your savings program this is. The consequences of constant disorganization over a year's time could cause significant losses to your savings.

Constant disorganization is a money drain. It will slowly leak away a few dollars at a time, and will add up over time. Minor disorganization, or losing something once in a great while will not add up significantly. Constant disorganization and lost time will add up over an extended period. It will cost you time and money. In a year's time, the cost of disorganization will become a significant reason why you were not able to save a substantial amount of money.

John Frugal and William Spendall.

Take our friend, William Spendall and his huge toolbox, for example, of how disorganization costs money. John Frugal was finally able to persuade William to learn basic repair and maintenance on his car and home (an excellent money saving technique). William went out and purchased various tools and a tool box. The problem, though, is William is not very organized. During one repair, he may misplace one or several tools. When the next repair job requires one of those tools, William is compelled to buy a second identical tool to finish the job. This is similar to compulsive buying. William would not need to buy the tool, if he were not disorganized.

Addictions Are Obstacles to Success

Another obstacle is addiction—not addiction to money, but to drugs, smoking, gambling, alcohol and other habits. An addiction devours everything, including time, family, self and money. Addictions block your path to save considerable amounts of money when you buy wants. They are also a detriment to success. Addictions often become the sole purpose of living; everything else is considered as worthless.

If you are addicted to something, you are more than likely a spender. Why? Because addictions burn money. Some take more money than others, but they all take money to support. An addiction is a time and money waster. Stop the addiction, start saving, and starting reaching for success.

Addictions are a very expensive want, so to save the most, they need to be eliminated. You may think you are saving a lot when you buy the cigarettes on sale, or buy the cheaper brand, but the savings are fruitless compared to the amount of what could be saved by eliminating the addiction altogether. The best way to save on wants—even addictions—is to use moderation and elimination. Coupons and sales may save 25 or 30%, but elimination of the addiction will save 100% all of the time.

A person can become addicted to anything. Do not think just because you do not smoke or drink you do not have an addiction. If you use, eat, or drink something excessively it is an addiction. Fat and over-eating are the results of an addiction to food. An excessively hyper child is probably addicted to sugar. Using medicine for every little thing when it is not necessary is an addiction. Anything can become addicting, and many people do have varying degrees of addictions. Some examples of addictions are:

• Food	• Sugar	• Caffeine
• Chocolate	• Salt	• Medicine (such as cough syrup or Asprin)
• Video games	• Sex	• Gambling
• Cigarettes	• Alcohol	• Phone

Gambling is the perfect example of how an addiction is a deterrent to reaching your savings potential. When you try to gain from a win/lose situation, in the end you will never come out ahead. You may win one gambling evening, but over time you will lose more than you will ever win. You will lose more than just money. You will lose time and energy. You may lose friends and family, and you may even lose your life. When gambling becomes an addiction, it will gobble up everything you have, including your savings, your automobile, your family and your life. Gambling is a serious addiction, and you should stay clear of it.

Another particularly bad addiction is talking on the phone. Long-distance phone bills can be staggering when there is an addiction to talking. Remember our friend, William Spendall? He is constantly on the phone—day in and day out, hour after hour. The worst part of it is he thinks he is doing business, but in reality it never brings in any money. Most calls are made because he is obsessed with talking on the phone. William's wife tries to change his obsessive habit, but to no avail. The irony is that William, when he sees the phone bill, calls it outrageous. William's wife finally ends up paying the bill, even though William is the culprit. You might think William, after seeing the phone bill would change, but he does not, because he is addicted. He does not realize *he* is the problem—and non-recognition is a clear symptom of addiction. The hard facts of the phone bill will not jog William Spendall, the addicted, into realization of his errors. In the end, his wife is finally forced to pull long-distance service from the phone. She is taking a drastic step to stop William's addiction.

An addiction is never good. If an addiction is taking over your money, eliminate it. Take the power and resources to get rid of it. It may be a difficult task, but it can be done. If you want to get rid of the addiction, get help. The first program does not work? Keep trying until you find something that does. It can be very hard to remove an addiction, but if you truly believe in yourself, and truly desire to reach success, the addiction can be eliminated. Spend some time and money to remove the addiction, the obstacle on your road to success, so you can reach success. The lost resources of time and money will easily be reclaimed by the ability to save the money now being spent on the addiction. The benefits in the long run will easily out number the withdrawal symptoms. Remove the addiction from your life so you can see clearly and move forward on your road to success.

When you buy wants, or unneeded things, there are many obstacles blocking you from saving. Many or only a few obstacles may block your road, but no matter what the quantity, no matter how big and impassable they may look, there is always a way to get through them. Your obstacle(s) could be just a small hole needing the courage to be jumped. Maybe the only obstacle holding you back is just to do it. Stop thinking of the hole as a canyon. Jump the hole and start saving. Overcome those obstacles blocking your path so you can start saving your way to success and start reaping the rewards.

Points to Ponder:

- Do not become a part of the crowd who spends their way to sorrow; rather become one of the few who saves to success.

- Begin living below your income level; live below your means. Use the greatest savings method, moderation and elimination, to increase your savings several-fold.

- Do not raise your standards by buying luxury or status-seeking material possessions, but rather raise your standards of saving money.

- Desire success, work wholeheartedly and enthusiastically, discipline yourself, and use all your effort to reach success.

- Obstacles are only an experience to help you learn to overcome the obstacles coming later.

- If you cannot stop doing it, you are addicted. Compulsive spending is a very dangerous addiction. It is like a cancer eating away at your potential until there is no hope for success.

- Stop lending money, or paying the tab, when the money or favor is never returned, and eliminate an obstacle to saving towards success.

- Become organized in your life, and begin saving money.

- An addiction to anything including food, alcohol, gambling, candy, or the phone, is an obstacle which, once removed, will save enormous amounts of money.

- Reduce how many wants and how many "needs" (which are actually wants) you are buying, and you will dramatically increase your potential for success.

**Become a doer of things rather
than a buyer of things.**

5
START SAVING WHEN YOU EARN YOUR FIRST DOLLAR

*"Do not discourage your children from hoarding,
if they have a taste for it;
whoever lays up his penny rather than part with it for a cake,
at least is not the slave of gross appetite."*

Samuel Johnson[1]

Start saving when you earn your first dollar. Start learning how to save! Start teaching your child how to save. It is never too early to start. It is never to early too learn how to become a success by saving money.

"Many things will make a mighty heap," wrote Ovid.[2] The earlier, the better. Begin with a few cents then turn it into many dollars and then turn it into a mighty heap of savings. Benjamin Franklin wrote: "Many a little makes a mickle."[3] Begin now! At first the reward will be small, but as new knowledge is acquired, more money earned, and more money saved, the small pile will become a mighty heap.

No matter your age or the age of your children, you and your children should be saving. The earlier the savings can begin, the better. The more years lived while saving money, the larger the "heap" will be. What if you are not young anymore? It does not matter. Saving can accomplish so much, if you put your mind to it. Certainly, a ten-year-old has more years to save then a fifty-year-old, but both can save their way to success.

Teach Your Children How to Save

Benjamin Franklin articulated: "If a man empties his purse into his head, no man can take it away from him. An investment in knowledge always pays the best interest."[4] Invest in your children's lives by giving them knowledge and teaching them how to use that knowledge to save. Knowledge is a great investment of both time and money. You should be investing your time, and teaching your children to invest their time to learn how to save. Do not save money *for* them, but teach them *how* to save. A Chinese proverb states, "Give a man a fish and you feed him for a day. Teach a man to fish and you feed him for a lifetime."[5] Teach your children how to save. Give your children the knowledge that will teach them how to be financially fed for life.

Anyone can save, but if your child starts when young, it is almost a guarantee of success. Why? Because your child will have his or her whole life to learn how to achieve success. Your child will have the best investment, knowledge, taught from an early age, thus receiving an investment that will reap enormous rewards. Knowledge will help him or her become a success. Your child will learn how to save, how to become successful and how to reach his or her goals.

When your children learn about saving, they get a head start in life. By learning how to save when young, your children will always continue to save. It is like the star athlete who begins practicing a sport at an early age; teach your children when young, and they will become star savers.

When children get their first money, the first lessons of saving should begin. Whether it be a gift, an allowance, or compensation for work, some or (even better) all of it should be saved. This will lead them down the road to where 25% to 50% savings of take home pay is possible when they are adults. Whether it be to save a dime out of a dollar or the whole dollar, saving will lead children down the road of frugality and prudence, and toward the very real chance of success. Do not let them spend money foolishly just because they are kids and they "need" to have fun, or because they are only young once. What do they learn from this other than how to spend money "burning a hole in the pocket?" Kids need to be kids, but spending a lot of money should not be a part of the equation. Kids should have fun, but to save even only ten cents of each dollar will amplify their chance for success, and years from now they will certainly thank you for leading them down the road of saving that brought them the success they have. You just cannot wait. Do not procrastinate until tomorrow when you can do it today. Start as soon as possible to teach your children the most important financial lesson in their lives: to start saving money early in life and never stop.

Why Your Children Should Begin Saving Early in Life

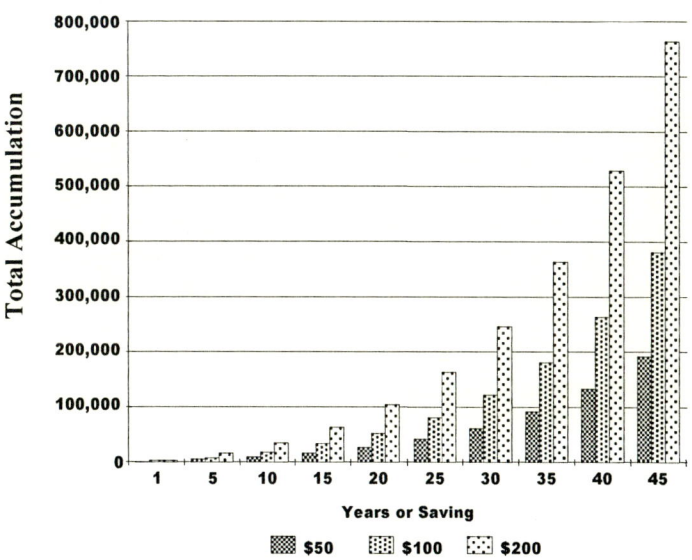

Why should your children start saving early? As indicated in the chart "Why Your Children Should Begin Saving Early in Life," by saving money over more years, you substantially increase your savings wealth. Compare the fifth year of savings ($50 per month at a 7% interest compounded monthly) which equals only $3,600.53 to the total forty years after beginning a $50 monthly savings plan. By the fortieth year, the savings has grown to an amazing $132,006.24! Starting your savings program early in life is a principle in the formula of saving your way to success.

Please take a few moments to examine this chart. It illustrates how saving more money per month (compare $50 to $100 and $200 per month saved) and saving over a longer period of time will greatly increase the amount of wealth you are able to accumulate. You and your children should begin saving now, not later.

Too Many Toys Teach the Wrong Attitude

How many toys do your children have? How many do they play with? How many were played with for a few days, then shoved away with so many others, never to be played with again? If toys are not being played with, why were they even bought? The money used to buy those unused toys could have been saved. It is a big area which could reap tremendous savings.

Many kids get far too many toys. They learn and believe that Santa is the real meaning of Christmas, and they get so many gifts and toys during the year that Christmas becomes a side show. Is there any meaning to birthday gifts when chidren get so many toys all year round? What does a parent teach a child when the child gets a toy every time he wants one? A spoiled child will become greedy, and will probably remain the same for life. Greed may bring riches for a while, but in the end, it only brings failure. Sure, children need toys, but do they need so many toys that they have duplicates, or boxes of toys they never play with any more? When spendthrift parents constantly buy toys, all children learn is how to take the toys, then ask for more, until it becomes a pitiful circle: want, want, want, take, take, take! Stop your children's craving for the new toys every week. Reduce your children's toy chest to the toys they will actually play with.

Rather than learning the right attitudes of how to handle money—how to become a saver—the child with too many toys will only learn how to become a spender. Too many toys create the wrong attitudes of money including greed and materialism. They will also teach a child how to become dependent. As a dependent adult, he or she will always be balancing on a line between a dependent life filled with debt and the abyss of financial ruin. Too many toys will create the wrong attitude—spending is better than saving. The child who learns this kind of an attitude will never reach success through saving; rather, he or she will spend his life in financial worries over bills, debt, and bankruptcy because too much of the income is spent on adult "toys."

Children and toys are inseparable. Toys are needed to help a child be a child. Too many toys, however, may produce greed, materialism and other negatives, including lack of self-discipline and self-confidence. Stop the toy spoiling and save the money for your child's future.

Saving is a Value You Can Teach Your Child

Saving should be a part of your child's growth. Saving can teach responsibility, morals, integrity, duty and endeavor. Teach your children to be responsible with their money. Teach that excessive spending can lead them down the road to disaster. As a child grows and learns math, English and history from school, and morals and manners from home, teach the value of savings as well.

Teach your children the value of saving. As a parent, you must teach your children to save so someday each child will become a success through saving. No one else is going to teach them. They may not learn how to save money at school, and they certainly will not learn about saving from most of their peers. If you do not teach them, who will? It is your responsibility. You have only one chance in each of your children's lives—when he or she is a child. Let me repeat this: *you have only one chance to teach your child the power of saving; that is, when your child is a child.*

A child who does not save, spends. As explained in chapter one, there is no alternative; your child is either a spender or a saver. Incorporate savings into their everyday life, rather than having your children become spenders. If your children learn only how to spend, they will only run into a whole gamut of money problems. Do not let your children become spenders; instead, teach them to become savers. Teach your children how to save their way to success.

Spending can turn a child into a materialist. The only thing that matters to a materialist is buying, whether it be because of want, money burning a hole in the pocket, or covetousness. Materialism is a downfall; it brings about corruption through want and spending. It forces a child into the idea that success and competition are based solely on who can have the most material things. "He who has the most toys when he dies wins," goes the saying. That is covetous. No longer are necessities being furnished. Food is scratched for "toys"; the family is forgotten. Even own personal needs including clothing are forgotten or displaced. Spending becomes an aberration. A drunk or gambler does not save, but spends. Spending can lead to all this. In contrast, saving can foster the good of a child. Rather than becoming a materialistic spender, a child can become a happy, self-reliant, financially independent, successful saver.

From the lesson of saving comes self-esteem, responsibility and economic well-being. Do not teach your children to become spenders, teach them the fruits of saving. Rather than buying them the new toy with five dollars, take the five dollars and save it for their future. Rather than allowing your children to buy whatever your children want, show them how to save the money. Saving is the value that builds the bridge to your children's success no matter what line of work they choose.

Saving Teaches Self-Reliance

Saving teaches self-reliance, and through that will raise self-esteem and enhance the ability to reach goals. Saving will teach responsibility, financial-well being, moral responsibility and self-esteem that together will add up to an impregnable self-reliant confidence allowing your children to invest in themselves, and reach their goals for success.

Saving can teach many things that will make a person become self-reliant. Saving can teach self-esteem that arises from doing something without being dependent on others and their money. It creates the self-reliance of being able to help oneself, without government or family support. It creates responsibility for one's actions and forces a person to be responsible for one's own needs rather than dependent on others. It can teach moral responsibility: the reasoning that material goods, including money, are not and should not be the number one thing in a person's life. Saving will teach financial well-being and make a person capable of handling any amount of money with assurance rather than being afraid of what to do with it. It lays the foundation for financial and personal success.

Saving Teaches Responsibility

Like chores and parental discipline, if saving is taught correctly, it will teach your child to be financially responsible. A 1992 survey of high school students, college students *and* the general public found that 64% could not define the word "profit."[6] By saving, your child will learn what a product is actually worth. The value and need of money earned morally and economically responsibly will also be taught.

Moral responsibility can also come out of saving, as children learn to define need versus wants. If your child saves ten dollars by buying a toy at a rummage sale rather than brand new, those ten dollars can be used to teach moral responsibility. It can be used as a donation, or can go to pay bills, or it can be saved. It can also teach a child about success and competition. It can teach that money is not everything, and you do not need enormous amounts of money to be successful, but you do need to save.

In the 12 months ended in March 2002, a record 1.5 million Americans declared personal bankruptcy—up 15.1% from the previous year.[7] Bankruptcy comes from covetousness. People may try to place the blame on something else; but bankruptcy comes from unpaid bills and loans. What were the bills and loans for? Money. Money to buy things. The bills were unpaid spending, and the loans were for money to spend. A plan for saving can help avoid most of these financial problems.

Saving is almost a guarantee against bankruptcy. If used wisely, efficiently and effectively, saving will be a 90% guarantee you will not go bankrupt. The more you save, the better guarantee you have. Of course, if you save little, and have numerous debts, there is not much of a guarantee. There is only a guarantee when there is strong savings and little or no debt. Savings can stop bankruptcy from happening, because savings teaches a person to handle money. A person will still have bills, and maybe even loans, but the person knows how to live within his limits. Bankruptcy becomes highly unlikely when saving is incorporated into the finances of a person's money and lifestyle. The person has learned how to save money, which will lead to financial self-reliance, and has not learned how to spend money extravagantly, which often leads to bankruptcy and financial ruin. When a person saves, the saved money becomes a cushion against any unexpected bills that may appear.

Never should a person be in a position to even consider the prospect of filing for bankruptcy. Adam Smith wrote: "Bankruptcy is perhaps the greatest and most humiliating calamity which can befall an innocent man."[8] Bankruptcy is financially very painful and disastrous. It stays on your record for seven years. If you desire to succeed, then you must eliminate even the *possibility* of bankruptcy.

All these are reasons your children should be taught how to save money—not only a little bit, but a lot. If taught how to save, your children will avoid "money trouble," including overburdening debt and bankruptcy, as adults. Saving will show your children the way to success. Do not wait on your children's future. Begin now to help them start saving. Saving can teach so much. Do not just teach your children to save, but teach them what saving can and will do for them.

There are no shortcuts to teaching the value of saving. As a parent, you should be constantly and consistently sharing with your children a profuse amount of saving knowledge, so saving will become a habit and they will save money all the time. Never stop the lessons. Begin as soon as possible. If your children are already grown up, or close to becoming adults, you will have to quicken the pace and teach as much as you can as fast as you can. Saturate their minds with the benefits of saving money. Never believe your children are too old to be taught something, especially something as important as saving. The lessons of life require an infinite amount of time; the lessons of saving need a great deal of time as well.

Allowances Can Turn a Child into a Saver or a Spender

Should you give your child an allowance? Allowances can and often should be used. Allowances can be very beneficial as long as your child is actually *earning* the allowance. Allowances teach work ethics, and can teach your child how to earn money and save money.

Zillions, the consumer magazine for children, conducted a survey of children around the country. According to the survey, children who do not receive allowances get access to almost as much money as children who do.[9] They get "free" money and they do not learn the ethics and responsibility that comes with work and earning money. These are the children who may grow up to be dependent on this "free" money. The same survey also found that children with allowances are happier with the amount they receive because they have more control over their money, and feel better because they do; they actually earned the money, without just getting "free" money.[10] Children who earned allowances will have increased self-reliance and self-esteem because they performed the amount of work necessary to accomplish the task and to receive the reward: the allowance. They are the children with the most self-esteem and the better chance of success in their future. The survey also found the children who earned money are also more likely to save money.[11] Earned money can be very beneficial, but "free" money never is.

If you want children who are proud of themselves, and will grow up proud, then do not give them "free" money and lots of gifts; instead, you should give them work and an allowance. Self-esteem comes from accomplishing something. When children win a game, or get a good grade, or create something in art class they like, they feel good about themselves. They accomplished something and they created self-esteem. The same feeling should come from an allowance. Do not give your children money; give them the chance to earn money. Do it right, and an allowance will give your child a boost of self-esteem.

Allowances can teach many things, but it all depends upon the teacher. You, the parents, must teach your children; do not rely on someone else to do it. Children may learn elsewhere, but it is up to you to start them out. They will learn the value of work, time, and money and the correlation between them when you, as parents, teach them. It will teach them to save versus to spend. It will teach them responsibility. It will teach them how to save toward success.

Teach the Lessons of Work, Time, Effort, and Money

How much time was taken to earn the money to buy a particular item? Your children should be learning how to answer this question as they get older. If they do not already know and understand the concept, then teach them the value of their time and work in relation to their earned money's purchasing power. With earned money, your children can start contemplating the value of the toys, clothes or other things they wish to buy in relation to their own money, time and work. When they do this, they will learn a lot more about what things cost and their correlation to the effort it took to make the money to buy the things. This will show how and why they should save more. Your children will be able to question, whether they are getting a good value for their dollar and relate this back to the work and time put into earning the dollar. With this powerful understanding, your children will be able to make better spending decisions.

Teach the value and correlation of work, time, and money with an allowance. Rather than have a set allowance, give varying amounts according to how much work has been done. Allow a special extra bonus for extra work not normally done. This will teach the value of work. Make sure your children know there are jobs they have to do that do not pay. This will teach charity and will prepare them for adult life, where everything they do will not pay money. Responsibility can be taught in correlation with all of these. If the work is not done, do not pay the allowance. If your child does not do his or her job but still gets the allowance, then the idea of something for nothing will form. This may progress into laziness and dependency. Make specific rules, and make sure your child knows if the job does not get done, the allowance is not there—but if he or she does exceptional work, or work without being told, he or she will get a bonus over the week's allowance.

While you are trying to teach the value of work, try not to always force jobs upon your children. Your children may not learn quite as well, if not at all, from forced jobs and saving. Of course, this depends upon the circumstances. If a child resists learning, the lesson will not be learned. The lessons need to be taught to learn how to add, subtract, multiply, and divide. It is the same with saving. It does not matter if your child does not want to, it needs to be learned to know and understand mathematics and to be successful. The same is with allowances and work. The lesson needs to be learned for the child to become successful. Teach your child the values of work and saving the money earned from the work.

Use variety to teach responsibility, saving, and work values. Delegate different jobs and degrees of allowances. Assign a job needing to be done that day or hour, along with another more time consuming and/or more strenuous job that does not need to be done for several days—but make sure to emphasize they both need to be done. Create different jobs to give your children responsibility and a chance to use their own imaginations.

Teaching a lesson is a big part of giving your child responsibility of work and allowances. Actively participate with your child. Integrate lessons into the work. If your child learns nothing, what is really gained? Constantly help your child learn how to save responsibly, the value of hard work, effort, time and money and to make astute financial decisions.

How I Did It

I was fortunate to learn the lessons of work, time, effort and money when I was young. When I was only in grade school, I had a part-time job. My family was living in a small apartment building which was part of a complex of six comparable buildings. While the other neighborhood children where playing, I was often helping the apartment buildings' manager. I was not able to do difficult work, but I still worked. Whether it was raking leaves, or helping move paint, gravel or tools, or cleaning hallways, I was there to help if I could. Sometimes I was not formally asked to help, but would find a way to help anyway. Many times the work I did, without being asked, was greatly appreciated, and I would be compensated for it. Do not wait for the work to come to you; rather, you must go and find the work. I may have only made five dollars for a few hours' work, but I knew I had five more dollars in my pocket because of it. I learned when I was young that with every finished job there was more money accumulating in my pocket!

Reward School Grades, but Not with Money

What about paying for good deeds and good grades? This is a horrible habit. It is the same as if you got paid for just doing a good job at work. You are supposed to do good work, not sloppy work, or you would probably be fired. Should your child do sloppy schoolwork? Certainly straight A's are not necessary, but your children should try hard to get good grades without expecting to get paid for it.

Try valiantly to find another, non-monetary means to teach the lesson of the importance of school and grades. For example, if your child, a B and C average student, gets all A's and B's the first semester, congratulate your child by making a special supper, or taking your child out to a favorite restaurant. Paying children to make good grades in school is never a good idea.

If you want to do something to show your appreciation for your student's exceptional grades he or she worked very hard to get, give a reward other than money. A reward for grades would be honor role status, and a certificate for reaching the goal. I also recommend getting your local paper involved to print honor role student's names in the local paper. This would be a lot more memorable reward than some money.

To teach a child how to talk, you start with the first words, and you do not give up. It is the same with saving. Start with the first money your child earns, and do not give up. You might even start before then. Start a fund, such as a savings account or IRA (Individual Retirement Account) for your newborn child. No matter how small the initial contribution is or how few times you contribute additional money, it will add up. The greatest advantage of starting a program of saving for your child is it will give him or her an excellent head start on saving. By the time your child is old enough to become responsible for the fund it will be a sizable sum of money. Your children will have a jump start on their success through saving because of the funds you started for them. As your children grow up, begin teaching your children about the savings you have procured for them. Remember: growth is better than no growth. Start on your children's future as soon as possible and never stop.

Progress with the lessons as your child progresses. Start with a savings plan even before your child is able to understand what money is. From there progress to letting your child save his or her own money in a piggy bank. Afterwards progress to a savings account and continue to progress as your child grows older. By the time your child is a teenager, gets a driver's license and begins his or her first job, your teenager will be fully prepared to reap the greatest savings in his or her life!

Points to Ponder:

- Knowledge is the best investment your children can ever receive. Do not save money for them, but teach them how to save their way to success.

- Toys are a part of children's lives, but too many toys will teach the wrong attitude that spending is better than saving their way to success.

- It is up to you as parents to teach your children the value of saving. Saving is in itself a value; it can teach self-reliance, raise self-esteem, teach responsibility, teach morals, and teach how to avoid financial disasters, such as bankruptcy.

- Saving will teach financial well-being and make a person capable of handling any amount of money with assurance rather than being afraid of what to do with it. It lays the foundation for financial and personal success.

- When a person saves a significant amount of his income, the person is creating a 90% guarantee against ever having to deal with bankruptcy and financial ruin.

- Allowances can teach a child to become a prudent, self-reliant saver, or they can teach a child to become a lazy dependent spender. It all depends on what values the parents teach when they use allowances.

- Never stop learning and teaching, and never wait until your children grow old. Begin now, and start your children travelling down the road of success.

- Use *Saving Your Way to Success* like a textbook to teach your child the principle of saving.

**The lessons of life require an infinite amount of time;
the lessons of saving need just as much time.**

6
THE TEENAGE YEARS

"He who hesitates is not only lost, but miles from the next exit."

Henry Ford[1]

The teenage years are the greatest opportunity to save up to 80%! If you are a teenager, you should be learning about saving. If you are a parent of a teenager, you should be teaching your teenager how to save. The teenage years are the years when the most money can be spent on wants, rather than needs; that is why they are also when the most money can be saved. The teenage years are by far the best opportunity in a person's life to save an enormous quantity of money. When saving becomes paramount, it will change the teenager's life forever.

In order to reach success through saving as soon as possible, a person should start saving as soon as possible. By beginning your enormous savings (by saving 80%) as a teenager, you will be able to reach success much sooner. If you hesitate, the time lost may cost you your success. Even if you hesitate only momentarily—by waiting until you are done with school, for instance—you will have a much more arduous time of reaching success. By spending, rather than saving, you miss two things: You miss out on several years of your life, so you will reach success much later. By waiting you have wasted time, which is the most valuable commodity on earth (see Chapter Ten). And you have missed out on the greatest opportunity to save as much money as you can. You will have missed out on the opportunity to save 80%! It is a a lifetime opportunity. There will never be another time allowing you to save so much of your income as the teenage years do.

Why is starting to save early a component to reaching success through saving? Examine the chart "How Much Savings Can You Accumulate?". Notice the significant difference of ten years' worth of savings compared to only five years' worth of savings. Then compare the ten-year number to the forty-seven year number. If you started saving $500 a month when you were only 18, continued to do so until the age of 65 (when you are possibly ready to retire) and received only 7% interest (compounded monthly) throughout all forty-seven of those years, you would have accumulated over 2.2 million dollars. Amazing!

How Much Savings
Can You Accumulate?

Per Month Savings at 7%

	$50	$100	$200	$300	$500
47	$220,600	$441,201	$882,403	$1,323,605	$2,206,008
46	$205,147	$410,294	$820,589	$1,230,885	$2,051,475
40	$132,006	$264,012	$528,025	$792,037	$1,320,006
30	$61,354	$122,708	$245,417	$368,126	$613,543
20	$26,198	$52,396	$104,793	$157,189	$261,982
10	$8,704	$17,409	$34,818	$52,228	$87,047
5	$3,600	$7,201	$14,402	$21,603	$36,005

(Years of Saving)

Per Month Savings at 5%

	$50	$100	$200	$300	$500
47	$113,685	$227,371	$454,743	$682,114	$1,136,857
46	$107,566	$215,131	$430,263	$645,395	$1,075,660
40	$76,618	$153,237	$306,475	$459,713	$766,189
30	$41,786	$83,572	$167,145	$250,717	$417,863
20	$20,637	$41,274	$82,549	$123,823	$206,373
10	$7,796	$15,592	$31,185	$46,778	$77,964
5	$3,414	$6,828	$13,657	$20,486	$34,144

(Years of Saving)

What else does this chart tell us?

- The more you save per month, the greater your total accumulation.
- If you double your savings per month, such as from $100 to $200 per month, you will automatically double your total wealth accumulation.
- By starting your savings accumulation early, and continuing it over a greater number of years, your savings will have a longer period to work the magic of compound interest; therefore, your total wealth accumulation will grow to a much larger sum.
- The better return you can generate for your savings, such as investing in the American Stock Market (8-12%) versus a savings account (2-4%), the greater your money will multiply.

Yes, it is true, saving can make you successful. By following the savings formula discussed in *Saving Your Way to Success* you can fulfill your dreams of independence, happiness and self-reliance. You will be able to create peace of mind and become financially independent.

In 2001, teenagers spent an average of $104 a week for a total of $172 billion.[2] Most of that money went to fast food, music, expensive clothes, movies, and anything and everything else teenagers want. Except for a few individuals, most teenagers' needs are satisfied by their parents or guardians. Most of a teenager's earned money is going to buy wants.

If you are the parents of teenagers, you should immediately begin the process of getting them to start saving money if they are not already doing so. Create within them the habit of saving, and they will have vested in themselves to become keen money handlers. They will have developed within their minds a subliminal message to think "save" rather than "spend." Of course, you can do this at any time in your life, but the amazing thing about the teenage years is it is so simple to save, that it creates a tremendous incentive to continue to save, and to create a habit of saving. This is why your teenagers should be taught how to save money—give them a copy of this book and have them read it, study it and use it as their personal money saving guide.

A teenager can save a lot of money, but first, a teenager must earn money. Send your teenager out searching for a job. It can be mowing lawns, delivering papers, or working at a restaurant. The sooner the teenager can begin earning, the sooner the teenager can begin saving.

A Teenager Must First Earn Money in Order to Save Money

In order to save money, your teenagers need to earn money. Do not give them "free" money; give them the courage and strength to earn money. Teenagers who still rely on allowances or "free" money from their parents will not have the practice and experience of the work force and will not know the real lessons of money and economics. Give your children the power to take care of themselves in the future.

A child does not learn math by getting the answers by copying or by having someone else, like the parents, do the work while the child sits passively. In order to learn math, the child must practice and solve the problems. Active thinking, not passive, improves the mind. The same is true with earning and saving money. Send your teenagers out to get a job so they will earn and save their own money. Teenagers who work while still living at home will have the experience and intelligence to get ahead of the others who live solely off their parents' income. Your teenager will be earning his or her own money, saving that money and learning while moving ahead in life.

The worst thing to do is to give your teenagers money. It is only "free" money and teaches nothing except how to become a dependent. Buying them things is the same thing as giving them money. "Free" money only teaches someone how to want more, ask for more, expect more, and take more "free" money. It teaches nothing else.

A job will teach the same things allowances do, except to a heightened degree. A job is preparing your teenager for the adult world. No longer are the lessons for a child, but for a teenager who is growing into an adult. It does not matter if your family is wealthy and your teenager does not "need" a job. A teenager needs a job to be able to learn about the real world. Your teenager will not be getting "free" money, so your teenager will need to get a paying job to learn how to live on his or her own when the time does come to become independent.

A job is almost as necessary in a teenager's life as school is. It teaches things school cannot. It teaches about real-life money and finances. It teaches about economics, business, and how the real world works. It prepares teenagers for the adult world. It teaches the value of money and hopefully, teaches them why they should save their money. Watch carefully, though, so excessive work does not begin to produce lower grades. Try to even out a nice mixture of job and school so your teenager reaps the benefits from both. Make sure school is first, but make sure your teenager is also learning from the job. Become the intermediary to make certain the mixture between school and work stays reasonable and the work does not become a burden.

A person should never wait for the "perfect" job. The person may be waiting a while. The smart individual who will get ahead faster knows a job is a job when it brings home a paycheck. Whether you are a teenager or a seasoned professional, if you wait around too long and remain out of the workforce, especially as you become older, it becomes very difficult to get back into the work force. For teenagers, this is not as much of a problem, but they should still not wait for the "perfect" job. Get a job as soon as possible. The job may not be great, but it is better than remaining idle and earning no money. Besides, once a job is acquired, it will look good on the resume´ and may help you get the "perfect" job or at least nearer to it. Not only teenagers, but everyone should respect the fact that the longer a person waits for the "perfect" job while not working, the farther the person slips away from the work force and of ever getting any job at all. Do not take a job you will completely detest, but sacrifice a little to get a job even if it is not "perfect." Take what you can get now rather than wait for the "perfect" job that may never come.

"As it is ridiculous not to dress, so is it, in some measure, not to be employed," wrote Adam Smith.[3] Never, never sit idle. If you are a teenager, by working, you will move closer to success no matter what job you work. And for an adult who loses employment, any job would be beneficial because it will at least keep you from falling away from your drive for success. To be unemployed for an extended period of time will always be detrimental to your drive for success. Invest in yourself and do what you have to do to acquire some form of employment so you can continue to move forward. *Never quit working; never wait for the "perfect" job. The time and money lost in idleness is a major detriment to reaching success. He who remains idle, remains poor in many ways.*

There are Many Benefits to Working

A job, no matter what it is, has benefits, especially the benefit of a paycheck. Would it not be better to have a paycheck that is something than not to have anything at all? The job may not be great, but turn it into something great. Show off your great working habits and skills. Always be a good, helpful worker. Use your imagination to make the work place better, more efficient and more exciting. Use your talents, abilities and willingness to work to get the higher pay you are looking for. Use all of these to get the boss's attention so you can get the raise and reference and move ahead. Use your mind to extract the benefits you want from the job, no matter what kind of job it is.

Work is good for the body and the mind. A teenager should have a job to gain experience to prepare for the working world. Experience is a good teacher. Encourage your teenager to continue and it will help prepare your teenager for the real world.

A job will boost your teenagers' self-esteem. They are accomplishing something. Your teenagers are earning their own money. "Free" money will not do that. "Free" money will lower his or her self-esteem. When the time comes to earn their own money to survive in the adult world, they will not be able to do it and self-esteem will flounder. If your teenagers, on the other hand, have learned how to earn money and to save money, they will be prepared for the adult world. Boost your teenagers self-esteem and let them earn and save their own money.

A job also helps boost self-esteem because it creates responsibility, and from that responsibility comes achievement. Who would not feel great after completing a job well done? If the person never tries at work, or becomes lazy, complacent or "does not care," then self-esteem will not be boosted immediately; but, if your teenager has a good boss who tries to infuse self-esteem and a positive mental attitude through responsibility and encouragement, the teenager will begin to reap the reward of achievement. Simply receiving a paycheck is an achievement and an incentive to keep working. If there is nothing else creating enthusiasm, growing self-esteem, or generating a more positive personality, getting a paycheck from "all the hard work" should at least receive a smile of satisfaction. No matter how you look at it, a job will generate encouragement and self-esteem.

A person who is working and saving at the same time will be able to move ahead of the person who is not working. The more money earned, the more can be saved. Hard work is the key to making money, and saving the majority of the earned money is the key to success. This is another benefit of a job. Looked back on after many years, no job will be regretted; every job helps increase total savings and helps you move closer towards success.

How I Did It

My first job when I was a teenager was at a fast-food establishment, Kentucky Fried Chicken. It was never even close to being a "perfect" job, but it was still work, and it carried several benefits I wanted. One reason I worked was so I would be able to afford to operate my car. Unless I was willing to use money I had been saving, I knew I had to acquire a part-time, after-school job. This was to help me learn about real-world income and expenses. It can do the same for your teenager. If your teenager cannot afford to drive an automobile, then you, as parents, should not step in and pay the bills; instead, let your teenager learn the valuable lesson of how important the paycheck really is. In fact, as a young entrepreneur, one reason I wanted a car was so I could drive back and forth to a part-time job. By getting the car, I made getting a job easier; and, since I had a job, I was able to operate the car.

The fast-food restaurant job was never completely favorable to me. As soon as the school year ended, I quickly switched to a better paying job that I liked better. Without the fast-food job, though, I probably would not have been able to operate my car and at the same time increase my total savings accumulation. Simultaneously, I learned about how bosses are, how to appreciate your boss, and how to do better work to please the boss and to get a raise. I also learned about tardiness, about customers and business, and about receiving a paycheck every two weeks. I may never use most of the information I learned from working there, and you may never use most of the information you accumulate from your first job, but I did learn the basics of what a real-world job is and how to succeed at it. The basic experience will always be a benefit in your life, even if you forget the specifics of the particular job. I will never regret working at the restaurant. I was able to move closer to my goal of becoming a success.

There are also jobs out there for teenagers which are often many times overlooked. During the same school year I worked at the fast-food restaurant, I also had another job at school. For only 15 to 20 minutes a day, I worked in the high school kitchen. I was not making a lot of money, but I was receiving a free lunch, which was costing $1.25 per day. For just a small amount of help needed every school day in the kitchen, I was able to save another $1.25 every school day towards my total savings amount. I was marching a little bit closer towards success.

Robert Frost wrote: "The world is filled with willing people; some willing to work, the rest willing to let them."[4] What category do you fit into? What category do you desire to fit into?

Do not become one of those people who will never accomplish anything in life and will always be a dependent because they do not work. Become a person who is willing to work hard, earn more money and save more money. Be the person who will become self-reliant, independent and happy because success has been reached. People who let others do the work may have it easy, but they will never have financial freedom, will never be independent, will never be self-reliant or have high self-esteem, and will especially never become successful. Be the person who is willing to work—to work toward success.

Get More Out of a Job Than Just a Paycheck

"Far and away the best prize life offers is the chance to work hard at work worth doing," said Theodore Roosevelt.[5] When you work, you need to get something out of it. Do work worth doing, not just mindless work to earn a wage. Sure, sometimes mindless work is the only work available. If so, any work is better then no work. *It is better to do mindless work for a short time than to become mindless by doing nothing for a long time.* From the mindless work you will have a better chance at getting a better job than the person who is mindlessly sitting on the couch watching television.

Try to accomplish more than just earning money when you work. Exercise the mind as well as the body. Use your mind to extract the benefits from your work:

- Learn.
- Experience.
- Increase your savings.
- Create friendships and business associates.
- Create good references.
- Move a step closer to success.

Maybe you have been stuck with one of those jobs that seems to be at the bottom of the barrel, and you are wondering how you are supposed to find work worth doing. Use your own ingenuity to turn your job into work worth doing. Maybe there is an idea you can create and use to increase productivity of yourself, a group of employees, or the whole business. Maybe you have an idea that could reduce expenses, including recycling byproducts or reducing waste. Maybe you could create a plan to increase the speed or productivity of something in the business. If you could just create a better relationship between the employees and the boss, or between the white and blue collar workers, you could change your own work for the better. You may possibly reap rewards including raises, additional benefits or an advancement in position within the company. By creating a plan and describing it to the boss, then implementing it, you will have created your mindless work into work worth doing.

The key with any job, no matter what it is, is that it can become a better job with the right attitude. If you desire passionately to acquire your paycheck, you will be able to find a way to make the job better. Be certain to learn as much as you can from the experience. Even mindless work allows you to save a part of your income. As long as you are willing to learn you will be able to extract something from a job, and you will be doing work worth doing.

Savings Knowledge Should Always be Expanding

After teenagers learn that work is the key to earning money, they can begin to learn that saving is the key to success. Stress the ideas:

- Hard work is the key to making money.
- Saving is the key to success.

Make sure your growing teenager learns these ideas and understands the differences. Make sure your teenager also understands that success does not necessarily mean enormous wealth, but enormous wealth can ensue after reaching success.

These basic ideas can make a big difference between success and failure for a growing young adult.

Never stop learning about how to save money and how it can become your key to success. Whether you are a teenager or not, the expansion of knowledge should never stop. During the teenage years, though, the increase in knowledge is critical, because the more teenagers learn and experience as teenagers, while under the umbrella of parental support, the better prepared they will be when they move away from the family into their own homes. The increase of knowledge should never stop, because knowledge is one of the ingredients you must invest in yourself (see chapter two) to attain your goals and dreams.

If your teenager has started young and has already learned the basics of saving and finances, then the next lessons may be very easy, but necessary. If your teenager is a spender, you need to start teaching saving immediately to stop the perils of careless spending. If you do not, chances are your teenager will be a spender most of his or her life. Start the lessons of saving early and give your teenager the knowledge to propel him or her to financial freedom, peace of mind and self-reliance.

A Teenager Can Save as Much as 80%

After teenagers are earning their own money, they can begin to save their own money. The benefits of saving will now be accessible to your working teenager. Your teenager will be able to have the potential to reach the goal of a savings of 80%!

By working and saving their own money, teenagers learn so much more than if you, as the parent, just save money for them. Doing something for your teenagers teaches them nothing except to be dependent on you. When teenagers learn how to do things, rather than passively watching someone else do it for them, they will then be able to do those things themselves. When teenagers earn and save their own money, they will be able to reap their own rewards.

The teen years are the best time to save because they are the years when the most can be saved. There is no better opportunity to save money than the chance for a teenager to save up to 80%.

Any teenager who has been spending all of his or her hard earned money on wants and does not have to buy needs, and who has the faith, will-power, courage and strength to change lifestyles and make it happen, can save as much as 80%.

The teenage years are the best time to save because, with a few exceptions, most teenagers do not have to worry about buying necessities. Most of their spending is going to wants. The best way you can save the most money is when you stop buying so many "things." Saving 80% is very possible for teenagers because "things," or wants, can easily be eliminated. The best way to save on those $150 sneakers or $15 compact disc is not to buy them at all. Eliminate and save up to 80%. *Grow the money you earn and do not spend it foolishly!*

Unfortunately, most teenagers spend their money on wants in order to be "cool." In order to save 80%, the designer jeans, new musical compact discs, new movies, and so forth need to, for the most part, be eliminated. The continuous, habitual spending of money on new fads, fancy "things," movies and music needs to be stopped. Wants can no longer be so profusely wanted. Forget the wants of today and think of what you want for your future.

It is a fact that "cool" and spending are "in" and financial well-being and saving are "out" for most teenagers. "People aged 12 to 22 believe in saving for the future, but relatively few are actually doing it," wrote Joyce M. Rosenberg in an aptly titled article, "Young People Save Saving for the Future."[6] In a 1992 High School Financial Awareness Survey by the College for Financial Planning, 60% of teenagers reported having a job. Of those with a job, the typical take-home pay, after taxes, per week was $80. The weekly savings of $80 per week take-home pay was a median of only $5—a measly 6.25% savings.[7] Why only 6.25% when it is very, very possible to save as much as 80%? Saving and finances are not being learned by teenagers who are supposed to be prepared by their schools for adult life. Why are our schools doing such a dismal job of teaching students how to be smart with their money? Saving is not on most teenagers' minds, although finances and saving should be, to help prepare for adult life and to have a chance to reach success.

As a parent, take charge and turn your teenagers into savers. Teach them that saving is the key to success. Teach them that being a part of the crowd does not yield any rewards. Individuality will make them stick out positively like a newly painted house on an old city block. Explain to them what saving can do for their future. Then explain to them what becoming a habitual spender will do to deter their plans for the future. Prepare them to be not just adults, but money saving, responsible, successful adults. Show your teenagers that "cool" is not life-smart, but working to earn money, saving money, and preparing for the future to become successful are what being life-smart is all about.

It is possible for a teenager to save up to 80%. It can be done. It has been done. If you are a teenager, you are missing out on a great opportunity to save money and get ahead. Do not wait until you are done with school; rather, start on your goals now! Waiting only delays your success, thus giving you less time to work on your goals. Start on your goals now with this awesome opportunity of saving a big percentage of money. Start cutting back on how many "things" you buy, and you will bring in good savings; drastically reduce how many "things" you buy, and you will bring in enormous savings. Any teenager can do it. You can do it. Put your mind to it, and you will be able to save up to 80%.

To achieve such great savings, smart-money management will have to take the place of being "cool." According to a survey of 1,176 students nation wide, 91 percent believed young people should save, yet the majority of them considered themselves to be spenders.[8] Forget about what others are doing; instead, use it as an incentive to get yourself to do what is best for your future. Think of how much money others are spending and how little they will be ahead when they finish school. Then compare it to the great advantage you will have because you have taken this once-in-a-lifetime opportunity to save so much money.

Anyone can reach his or her maximum savings potential, but a teenager has the possibility to achieve the huge savings of 80%. You can do it! Do not let anyone get in your way. Do not let spenders tempt you away from your goals: 80% savings, smart-money management and success. Do not rely on anyone else to get the job done for you. Rely only on your own initiative. As a teenager, you have the power to achieve 80% savings. Start now!

Points to Ponder:

- For whatever reasons that may emerge, do not hesitate in your drive for success through saving.
- A teenager must first earn money to save money; therefore, it is essential that your teenager has some type of work.
- Never quit working and never wait for the perfect "job." The time and money lost by idleness is a major detriment to reaching success.
- A teenager will gain many benefits from working a regular job: more self-esteem, exercise of the mind and the body, being able to afford a car or other things the parents do not provide, gaining experience, learning about real-world jobs, and moving one step closer toward success through saving.
- Become a person who is willing to work toward success. Do not allow idleness to consume your life. It is better to do mindless work for a short time than to become mindless by doing nothing for a long time.
- Do work worth doing by changing your detested, "mindless" job into a job you will enjoy. Change the work atmosphere and/or habits at the workplace by using your creative imagination.
- Never should you stop saving, and never should you stop learning about saving, especially during the teenage years.
- The greatest opportunity to save money is during the teenage years; because teenagers can save as much as 80% of their take home pay. All of the necessities are provided by the parents; therefore, all of the teenager's money, if not going to buy wants, can be used toward success through saving.
- The best time to start saving is early in life. If you are a parent, teach this to your children. If you are a teenager, start your savings program now.

He who remains idle, remains poor.

7
YOUR SAVINGS PROGRAM

*"In all things, success depends upon previous preparation,
and without such preparation there is sure to be failure."*

Confucius[1]

What is a savings program? A savings program is a specific
plan of action you have created to meet your specific needs. It is
created around your unique personality to bring you success
through saving. A savings program is not some set program that
cannot be altered. Nor is it a plan some "expert" has created that
will work for everyone. It is a program set up around specific
ideas and facts, but molded specifically to what your personal
needs and wants are. No specific program will work for
everyone. You are about to find out how you can create your
own personal savings program.

A Savings Plan Is Your Strategy for Reaching Success

A savings program is something you create to fit your own
personal needs and wants. A savings program is something you
have formed and set in motion to obtain for you your maximum
savings potential; and reaching your savings potential will bring
you financial freedom, independence, happiness and peace of
mind.

A savings program is a working plan helping you save
money. You collect information, ideas, and methods about
saving money; you combine what can be used, then start doing it.
A personal savings program is a program molded around your
own needs and desires created from money saving methods,
techniques and ideas that will work for you. When you create a

savings program you are taking the time to develop a plan to strive for success. When you create a savings program you will have a definite plan of how you will reach success.

Only you can create your own savings program. Take the ideas you can use and form them into your own savings program. As an adult you cannot use the savings method of not buying necessities, because you are buying your own necessities now. Scrap this method for your own personal savings program, but do not forget it. Remember it so you can pass it on to your teenager. Bring together the many other methods and ideas about saving you can use. Not everyone can use the same ideas, nor does the same idea produce the same results for every person who tries to use it. A person living in an apartment cannot use methods to save the cost of owning a house. A person who does not eat out often cannot use a method to save while eating out. Only you can formulate your own personal savings program that will accomplish what you want it to accomplish. You hold your own destiny. Sir Richard Steerle, an English essayist and playwright, said: "Every man is the maker of his fortune."[2] No one can make your fortune. Only *you* can make *your* dreams come true.

John Frugal and William Spendall

John Frugal and William Spendall, our two opposite friends, are perfect examples of the importance of a savings program. John is constantly and consistently able to save enormously more than William, because John has set in place a program he formed to fit his lifestyle and maximize his savings. William, on the other hand, never took the time to create a plan for what his goals were and how he was going to accomplish those goals. William never took the time to acquire a wealth of knowledge. He never took the time to start an income and expense record book. Because of his inability to create a savings plan, William is only able to save haphazardly; consequently, he never has a consistent and measurable amount of savings. Because of his inconsistent, minute savings, William will never reach success through saving.

> Remember: by creating a personal savings program and following it enthusiastically and wholeheartedly, you will be able to use saving as the key to success.

A savings program consists of specific goals, dreams and savings methods composed together to maximize what can be saved. Think of it as a plan. Without a plan, you may wander about, not knowing where you are going, how to get there, or where you even need to go. These are all negative hindrances impeding your progress. A savings program eliminates all these negatives. By creating a savings plan, you put down in writing what you want, what you have now, how far you want to go, where you want to go and what methods are going to take you there. Like a military strategy to take a military position, this is your plan to reach your objective. Your specifically tailored savings program is your strategy for maximizing your savings potential so you can reach success through saving.

Every person needs to create a personal savings program. There are no set rules on how to create a savings program, or on what needs to be incorporated into it. There are, however, a few vital steps, or tools, that should be used. They will help tremendously in creating the perfect savings program specifically tailored to your needs, wants, goals, dreams and success. These steps will help you create your own personal savings program.

A Wise Saver Needs a Reality Check

First, begin an account book of all your income and expenses. Write down every dollar you spend and earn. Include everything: your checking and savings accounts, cash, credit cards, your regular wage and any other money you may receive, such as income from side jobs. Include every dollar and every cent. Until you have mastered how to save money, every cent recorded in your account book will be significant. Those dimes and nickels can add up after a period of time. Rather than breaking dollars, use your cents to buy snacks, pop and small expenses to simplify your record keeping. Once saving has become a natural habit, you should be able to remove the cents from your record keeping because you will have mastered how to save money and maximized your savings potential. Until that time, though, to help you reach your savings potential, keep track of every dollar and cent.

An account book has many benefits. It details what you need to do. It gives you an accurate picture of what you are currently spending and saving, and it divulges to you what you need to change to get the savings you desire. You will now realize where your money is going. You will be able to decide what you can eliminate, what can be reduced, and what will save you the most money. With an account book and all its benefits you will be on your way to success.

An account book, or a record of income and expenses, will allow you to realize what your efforts have produced. If you have reached a 10%, 20%, or 30% savings, your records and a little arithmetic will give you the proof. An expense record book will help you on your journey to huge savings. You will be able to watch your progress grow as you save more and more and know when you can reach 50% savings and finally have reached it.

An account book allows you to examine how you are spending your money. Do you have a monstrous expense, including an addiction to candy and chocolate, or an inclination to eat out all the time, eating and continuing to eat at your income like a hungry monster? By examining your account book, you will be able to discern where your money has been going and then be able to eliminate any superfluous expenses.

An account book will be able to help you remove those painful credit card debts. By creating a record of your income and expenses, you will be able to spot the crack in the hull of your financial ship before it grows too large and sinks you to the bottomless abyss of debt.

Take a few moments now to begin your own income and expense record book. Examine the two examples of a monthly income and expense report. Which format would you be able to use the most? Which format would be the easiest for you to work with? Decide which format would better suit your needs. Once you have made this decision, grab either a clean 3-ring notebook or an account ledger book (available at any office supply store) and begin immediately your own personal income and expense record book.

An account book is your personal progress report. It is your own personal positive helper. As long as you continue to grow your savings, it will show your amazing, positive results, and if at some moment you lapse in your savings, it will exhibit this fact to you, but will still reveal to you the amount and percentage of what you did save. When you start out down the road of savings, the account record book will be your map showing you if you are on course, steered off, or completely lost. Use the account record book to navigate your way through the rough detours and obstacles impeding your way to reaching your goal of maximizing your savings. You will be able to watch your savings grow, grow, and GROW!

Example 1 of a Monthly Income and Expense Record Book

	3/1	3/4	3/5	3/7	3/8	3/10	3/13	3/14	3/15
Income		$1,234.							
Savings			$123.0						
Automobile			$100.3			$15.00			
Clothing						$145.5			
Housing					$43.40				
Food	$26.42			$34.87		$4.16		$75.89	$6.18
Misc.							$250		
Leisure				$52.30					

	3/16	3/17	3/18	3/20	3/21	3/22	3/22	3/23	3/24
Income			$1,413						
Savings				$142.0					
Automobile		$20.00							$20.00
Clothing									
Housing								$67.80	$890.
Food	$3.77			$16.45	$24.75	$163.3			
Misc.	$28.80								
Leisure		$16.34		$37.32			$50.90		

Example 2 of a Monthly Income and Expense Record Book

Date	Transaction Description	Amount	Running Total
3/1	Bought Friend Dinner	$26.42	$344.58
3/4	Paycheck	$1,234.62	$1,579.20
3/5	Savings Fund	$123.00	$1,456.20
3/5	Car Brake Repair	$100.32	$1,355.88
3/7	Cable Bill	$52.30	$1303.58
3/7	Take Family out to Eat	$34.87	$1268.71
3/8	Electric Bill	$43.40	$1225.31
3/10	Fast Food Lunch	$4.16	$1221.15
3/10	Gas for Car	$15.00	$1206.15
3/10	New Outfits	$145.56	$1060.59
3/13	New Com. Printer	$250.00	$810.59
3/14	Groceries	$75.89	$867.70
3/15	Fast Food Lunch	$6.18	$861.52
3/16	Fast Food Breakfast	$3.77	$857.75
3/16	Car Payments	$723.00	$134.75
3/16	Tools for Work	$28.80	$105.95
3/17	Gas for Car	$20.00	$85.95
3/17	Music CD	$16.34	$69.61
3/18	Paycheck	$1,413.45	$1,483.06
3/20	Savings Fund	$142.00	$1,341.06
3/20	Telephone Bill	$52.33	$1,288.73
3/20	Buy Videos	$37.32	$1,251.41
3/21	Lunch and Dinner	$16.45	$1,234.96
3/22	Family Movie Night	$50.90	$1,184.06
3/23	Eating out	$24.75	$971.22
3/23	Groceries	$163.34	$995.97
3/23	Restaurant	$24.75	$971.22
3/23	Water, Gas	$67.80	$903.42
3/24	House Payment	$690.45	$212.97

Define Your Goals by Transforming Them into Substance

You need to know where you are going. To do that, you will need to examine, contemplate and decide where you want success to take you. This next step may or may not be tough to accomplish. Take as much time as you want to think about your dreams and goals; then, you must write them down. By putting them on paper, you turn your thoughts into substance. This is the second step in creating a savings program.

When you write your goals and dreams on paper it gives them form and substance. They will always be there. If they are on paper and always somewhere where you will see them constantly, they will be like a force compelling you to take action to accomplish those goals and reach those dreams.

There is a proven value to the concept of written goals. Yale University graduating seniors participating in a study about goals points out the significance of written goals. Only 3% had specific written goals. 10% had goals, but had not given them substance. The remaining students had no specific goals. Resurveyed twenty years later, the 3% group was so much more successful they outperformed the combination of all the others.[3] Giving goals substance motivates you to take action to reach those goals.

You will never have a reason not to work on your goals when they are in material form. By writing goals down, you are more apt to get started in accomplishing them. If you are a person who sometimes procrastinates, or someone who forgets things, than you are a person who especially needs to write your goals on paper. By taking some moments to write your goals and dreams on paper, you make yourself think and focus on your dreams and goals. *Dreams are only dreams until you give them life. By writing them down you have given them form and substance; rather than just being wild dreams or fantasies, those dreams become goals with a solid plan to achieve.*

Write your dreams and goals on a piece of paper and keep it easily accessible, so it becomes a tool for your success. As you move toward those goals, you will be able to use the list as a reference to see how you are progressing. Once written down, goals are set. They cannot be moved ahead of your progress. Certainly goals can be changed, but by writing them down you may be less apt to move them ahead before you reach them, depriving yourself of the awesome happiness and satisfaction of actually reaching a goal. Once goals are reached, make new ones. By writing them down you know how your progress is, have less tendency to change them as you come close to reaching them and you will know when you reach one of your goals.

By writing your down you are forced to think about them. It also forces you to start taking action. As you move along you will be able to look back at the paper containing your dreams and goals and check your progress. Change some of the goals as they no longer fit your wishes. Maybe you have accomplished some, and have new ones to reach for. Like the account book, writing your dreams and goals on paper serves as a road map. It shows you where you want to go. It gives you your destination.

Knowledge is Your Means of Moving Forward in Life

Now that you have your maps and your destination, you need the means to get there. The next step is just as crucial as the first two: to find out as much as you can about how to save money. Find the best money saving methods and techniques, such as those discussed in *Saving You Way to Success*. Learn as much as possible about saving and never stop searching, finding and learning more information about saving, or anything you desire to accomplish. The methods and ideas you learn are your means of getting where you want to go. Collect as much information as you deem necessary to formulate a plan for your success.

Never, ever stop accumulating knowledge. Even when you have created a savings program, and even after you have reached success, you should continue gaining new knowledge. There will always be new or improved ideas, and unless you continue to increase your knowledge, you may never know about them. Do not get stuck with older equipment. Expand your capacity and capability to always learn more new information. Unless you always continue to expand your knowledge you will never be able to use those newer, better ideas when they do come out. You must learn as much as you can about saving and your work. The day you quit learning is the day you quit moving ahead.

Reading and accumulating knowledge are keys to formulating the best plan for success. Read as much as you can about saving, and never stop learning, because the opposite of knowledge and learning is ignorance. Knowledge is a great wealth builder. The more you know, the better you will be able to make decisions; consequently, the more successful you will become. The more you know, the better able you will be to know how to reach your success. The more you know, the better savings program you will be able to create. Write down and remember all the ideas and methods you can use. Gather as much knowledge and information you can about saving and then use your powerful mind to create your successful savings plan.

By reading *Saving Your Way to Success* you are already gaining knowledge. Congratulations! By reading this you are now one step closer to success! This is your transportation to your destination. The constant accumulation of methods, ideas, and information about saving is what you will use to attain your goals. You already have your map, and know where you want to go, but by accumulating all this information you know how you are getting there. Napoleon Hill wrote: "Knowledge paves the road to riches—when you know which road to take."[4]

Reach Your Goal by Taking Action Immediately

After acquiring the knowledge and putting it all together, you need to implement it. Take action! Ben Franklin wrote: "Never put off till tomorrow what you can do today."[5] This is what you need to do. No matter what else you have done, it simply does not matter until you take action. Stop putting it off. Stop saying you will begin tomorrow so you can start reaching toward success today!

After all the above steps have been taken, the only thing left to do is to do it. Take your wealth of knowledge and start using it. Put everything to use. Take the methods and ideas you have decided to use and start using them. If they are not used, then all of your knowledge building was a waste of time. The person who gets ahead is the person who decides to move forward by taking action. Put to use what you have learned in *Saving Your Way to Success* and start accomplishing, rather than just thinking about accomplishing. Move ahead decisively. Take your knowledge of the many methods and ideas of saving you have amassed and start using them so you can start saving money and start fulfilling your dreams and achieving your goals. Determine what your destination is, take the road map, get in your power vehicle, and begin to drive toward your success.

After all these steps are taken, only then will you be on the road toward success. Along the way change your means of transportation if you find something better. Change your plans, if necessary, but never sway from your goals, or you will never reach them. Possibly, you have found a better method than what you are currently using. Grab the new method and run with it. Never constantly change your goals, though, or you will never be able to reach them. If something is not helping you reach your goals, change your plans to something that will. Remember: the person who never tries, will not succeed, but the person who continues to try will.

Your Personal Savings Program Will Procure Success for You

By following the steps for setting up your personal savings program, then investing in yourself, and finally, taking action, you will reach success. Believe in yourself. Desire to reach your goals, discipline yourself to use all your effort and time wisely, work wholeheartedly towards your goals, and do so enthusiastically. Then after investing in yourself, you need to develop your own personal savings program through creating an account book, planning out what your goals are and how you are going to reach them and acquiring the knowledge that you need to accomplish your goals. After you have done all this, you need only take action and success will be yours.

Without a savings program, you may very well not reach success through saving. Saving is the key to success when a person saves continuously and wholeheartedly. *A meager savings does not procure success, it only procures a meager savings.* By creating a savings program allowing you to maximize your savings, you will be able to grab the key to success.

You now know how to create your own savings program. Start working on it now! By reading this book you are already taking one step toward creating and implementing your own personal savings program. You are already on your way towards success! Start working on your savings plan as you continue reading *Saving You Way to Success*. What you may only need to do now is to take action. Many people fall at this step, but you will not! Move ahead! After all, you have started an account book, decided what your goals are and written them down, gathered information and decided what ideas and methods to use, and have put it all together to take the final step. Start saving! Start succeeding!

The steps described in the previous parts of this chapter were a simple, proven way to create your own personal savings program. Implement them to reach success. You need to take these steps and use them to create your own personal savings program.

Have you now taken all four necessary steps for creating your own personal savings program?

Step 1: Create your own monthly income and expense record book.

Step 2: Give your goals substance by first deciding on your goals and then writing them down on paper and displaying it somewhere where you will see it every day.

Step 3: Acquiring the necessary knowledge on how to save and invest your money to help you reach your goals.

Step 4: Take action immediately and implement your savings program so you can begin maximizing your savings potential and reach your goals.

There are several crucial steps you need to take to begin saving correctly by maximizing your savings potential. By creating your own personal savings program you have completed step one. The next chapter will explain the remaining four steps you need to implement in your drive to maximizing your savings potential in order for you to save correctly by saving as much as you can as fast as you can.

Points to Ponder:

- Your specifically tailored savings program is your strategy for maximizing your savings potential so you can reach success through saving.
- Only you can create your own savings program because every individual's desires and lifestyles are different.
- An account book is your tool for descrying what you need to do in order to save the amount of income you have set as your goal.
- Dreams are only dreams until you give them life. By writing them down you have given them form and substance; rather than just being wild dreams or fantasies, those dreams become goals with a solid plan to achieve.
- You will not be able to reach success unless you have the knowledge to get there. By acquiring as much knowledge as you can from reading and other means, you will know how to reach success.
- Nothing, absolutely nothing, will help you reach success, unless you begin taking action on the knowledge you have learned, taking action on the goals you have set, and changing your saving and spending habits as presented in your account book.
- By following the steps in this chapter to set up a savings program, by investing in yourself, and then by taking action, you will reach success.

**A meager savings does not procure success,
it only procures a meager savings.**

8
FIVE STEPS YOU NEED TO TAKE

*"Get what you can, and what you get hold;
'Tis the stone that will turn all your lead into gold."*

Benjamin Franklin[1]

Save as much as you can, as fast as you can, and propel yourself forward to success through saving. That must be your first objective in order for saving to be your key to success. If you wait, or if you hold back from maximizing your savings, you will reach financial success at a much later date (if ever). Start now, and quickly work yourself to the point where you have maximized your savings, and you will reach success not in decades, but in only a few years.

You need to remember—saving is the key to success when you are saving at your maximum potential, such as 25% or 50%, not at a measly 5%. Reach your maximum savings potential by taking the following steps:

Step 1: Create your personal savings program.
Step 2: Work more and harder.
Step 3: Changing your habits from a "spender" to a "saver."
Step 4: Never stop saving money.
Step5: Using your opportunities of opportunities.

Step One: Create Your Personal Savings Program

In the previous chapter, we outlined step one in achieving your objective of saving as much as you can, as fast as you can. If you have not set up a personal savings program, you should stop reading and complete this task now—before you move on in this book! Once you have set your goals, created an income and expense report, gathered ideas, methods, and techniques of how to save money, and have disciplined yourself to follow your personal savings program, you will have to take the following additional steps in order to *maximize your savings.*

Step Two: Work More

After setting up a personal savings program, the second step is to create more income. In order to save money, you first need to earn money. If you already have a job, great! If you do not, you need to get one—immediately!

Start earning your *own* money so that you can save your *own* money to make your own future. Do not depend on other people to make it possible for you. We talked about this in chapter six: working is always beneficial. Work is more than just earning money. It is an invaluable teacher as it prepares you for the future. If you missed the reasons to get a job, read chapter six again. A job is the key to the beginning of huge savings and success potential.

"Any man who has a job has a chance," Wrote Elbert Hubbard.[2] If you do not have a job, you will not have a chance to save money, and you will not be able to save your way to success. Work alone will not make you successful, but by working, you have accomplished the first task in the process of reaching success.

If you already have a job, great! Now you need to begin working more. By increasing your income, you will be able to save more. Take the opportunity to work over-time when it is available. Begin to work a part-time job to increase your income. You need to discipline yourself to begin working more so you can begin earning more.

You have only three choices of how to increase the size of your bank accounts:

- Save more.
- Earn more.
- Save *and* earn more.

By deciding on choice number three you will move forward twice as fast then if you were only increasing your savings or increasing your income. This is why step two is crucial to maximizing your savings potential.

Step Three: Saving Should Become "Cool"

The third step, just as crucial as all the others, is to make "coolness" second to saving. You do this by changing yourself from a "spender" to a "saver." Saving may force you to do some things that are not "cool," or not do things that are "cool," but it will bring about success. Stop worrying about being "cool" and start worrying about your future. Put saving, your future, and success first as your number one priorities over being "cool."

All to often, spending is considered "cool", while not spending (saving) may be considered "uncool." To become a saver you need to give "cool" the second seat to allow saving to be your number one priority. Name brand jeans, expensive cars, and music are all bought with the thought of being "cool." Instead, everything needs to be reduced and some things may need to be eliminated to succeed in your savings program.

Spending to be "cool," to keep a particular status quo, to seek status, to keep up with the Joneses or to live beyond your means all mean the same thing. What you are doing is spending money to impress others. In order to save money, you will need to change this habit. Spending to impress others *may* impress the neighbors, but it will *not* help you reach success.

One example of changing yourself from a "spender" to a "saver" is reducing your name brand clothing purchases. The best method to save money on your clothing purchases is to shop for good used clothing at garage sales or clean second-hand stores. Also, you need to stop buying name brands for which you are basically paying for hype and not quality. Buy the $20 dollar jeans instead of the $60 dollar name brand jeans. You need to cut out name brand buying, because it is only a waste of money. As long as both products are quality products and the only difference is the name, there should be no reason to buy the name brand item. What really makes a name "cool" anyway? Can one name be more "cool" than another? Why not buy what will look nice and last, rather than buy the name brand that is "cool" and just a fading fad?

Teenagers and clothes are a perfect example of spending to impress. Many teenagers think they need the newest trendy clothing every year. In the fall of 1994, *Business Week* reported that the nation's 28.5 million teenagers, along with their parents, spent close to $9 billion dollars on clothes—about half of their total annual clothing tab[3]. The assumption that teenagers or anyone need every new clothing fad is going to have to be erased. You can reap huge savings by reducing how many clothes you buy.

Like clothing, automobiles are another consumer good for which many people spend beyond their means to impress or show off to others. Whether it is the teenager in high school with the fancy hot rod, or the middle-aged working husband and wife with the fancy luxury car and SUV, it is all the same—they are spending money to impress others.

Forget the expensive automobile and remember your future. Unless you are already wealthy, self-sufficient, and financially independent, you need to wait to buy a new automobile. When you are saving your way to success, you must be constantly living below your means, with no exceptions. "Does this mean I have to use an old rust heap?" you may be wondering. Absolutely not! You can have a very nice looking automobile in mechanically good condition, and save money at the same time!

An auto, as transportation, is necessary. It helps you get to work, school, business, and everywhere else. It should not be eliminated. Not to have a vehicle at all may even become a detriment in today's fast-moving society. The solution is not to do without an automobile, but to do without an expensive one.

There are alternatives to having an expensive new car. One solution is to simply buy a good quality, mechanically sound, used automobile. Search local newspaper classifieds. Begin to look around local used car dealership lots. Sooner, rather than later, you will find a good, quality, used automobile at a reasonable price that will save you lots of money.

Several important points to remember when shopping for a used automobile:

- A well-known used car dealership may be more truthful than an independent seller when it comes to questions on the mechanical condition of the automobile, but there is always the exception. Always be careful for the car dealerships out there that are trying to rip consumers off.
- If you are knowledgeable about the mechanics of automobiles, or know somebody who is and could help you, then you pretty much eliminate this worry when buying a used automobile. In fact, you would be better off buying from an individual seller. An individual may have more room for haggling the price lower, may lower the price for cash, and/or may be more grateful for a sale, rather than trying to get a set price for a profit (like a dealership would).
- When you are in the market for a used automobile, always be cautious. Shop around. Become aware of what area prices are for the make(s) and model(s) you are looking for. You must be patient. With a new car, you can walk into the dealership, and drive away with the car you want the same day. When you are looking for a used car, you may not find the car you are looking for with a reasonable price right away. It may take weeks or months. You will have to remain flexible and cautious, but always remember, in the long run, you are saving an enormous amount of money.

Step 4: Never Stop Saving Money

It could be financially suicidal not to continue the savings program you have created. To quit saving, at any time, even if you do become rich, may be financially disastrous. If you quit saving money, and start spending all you earn, the savings you had accumulated will slowly evaporate as unexpected bills eat your savings away. Once the savings have vanished completely, you will be unprepared when unexpected bills emerge. If you are unable to squeeze by, you will go into debt, which is the forerunner to bankruptcy, which is the same as financial suicide. Enormous income does not ever mean you are financially independent; rather, if saving is not there, an enormous income may mean you are hazardously balancing between debt and bankruptcy. To quit saving for any extended time may cause financial ruin.

Saving should become a part of your life forever. In fact, by the time you do become rich, you will be so accustomed to saving that it will probably remain a part of your life, even when you theoretically no longer need to save. Your savings program should become one of those habits that remain for the rest of your life. Savings is so financially important to getting ahead in life, that it should be started at once, no matter how old you are, and then never stopped.

To continue to make saving the key to your success, you need to always continue maximizing your savings potential. A person cannot simply save as much money as possible up until a certain point, then stop saving, and expect to be successful the rest of his life. Thomas Edison stated it eloquently: "Many of life's failures are people who did not realize how close they were to success when they gave up."[5]

You must continue saving in order to enjoy the fruits of success. If the saving stops because you are buying a house, or because you get married and are having a baby, or because you have a costly bill to pay, or any of dozens of more reasons that have become excuses for not saving money, then saving will never bring you the success you desire. Saving will secure for you financial freedom, independence, self-reliance, happiness, and peace of mind if, and only if, you invest in yourself to follow your savings program through good times and bad. Do not make any excuse for discontinuing your saving indefinitely. If you do, you also postpone indefinitely, your success. Become one of the few who can reap the rewards of a lifetime of saving; become one of the few who can enjoy the fruits of personal success.

Warren Buffet, during a stay at New York's Plaza Hotel, displayed his reluctance to spend profusely, asking a friend,

"Could you bring over a six-pack of Pepsi? You cannot believe what room service charges."[6] One of the richest men in America, Buffet, has not stopped saving money. If one of America's richest men cannot find a plausible excuse to halt his saving, how can you? As long as you are saving, you will be moving ahead in your quest. If the saving stops, so too will your success. Warren Buffet understands the compound interest principle of saving money and investing. If you save more (and invest wisely) you will earn more. If you do not spend those new earnings, you will be able to save and then invest them, completing the circle of compounding interest. Now your amount compounds indefinitely as it grows larger and larger by baby steps, small steps, then big hops, and finally enormous leaps. Is there any reason not to save money? No, absolutely not!

And you should save no matter your income level. If a person is desolate and poor, the person needs to save to start getting out of poverty and return to his or her dreams. If a person is not on the streets, but still "poor," meaning below the government's poverty income cut-off, then it is a prime opportunity and reason to save money. If a person is in the middle class, the person should still be saving to give him or her financial security. If a person is already in the upper class, then saving will get the person even further up the ladder of life and probably will make the person a millionaire or multi-millionaire. There is never a time not to save. Every time is the right time to be saving money.

Step 5: The Opportunity of Opportunities

Maybe you have been asking yourself, "How can I save my way to success when I am nearing retirement?" Or maybe you have been wondering, "How can a person who does not have 20, 30 or even 40 years available to save money reach success through saving?" "Have I missed all the saving opportunities of years gone by?" you may be wondering. You may be frustrated that you have missed prime opportunities to save money. Do not despair! There is one opportunity that is not time based, and does not pass any one by. It only takes reaching out your hand to grab it. It is always there waiting for you to grab it. The fact is, this opportunity, which stands alone, *is the best opportunity there is!* It is the opportunity of opportunities.

What is this opportunity of opportunities? You! Yes, *you!* All of the opportunities that may pass you in your life mean nothing if *you* possess the courage, the strength, the will-power, the ability, the decisiveness to move out of the crowd, and descry other opportunities that are still out there and grab them. Even if you have already missed prime opportunities in your life, it means relatively nothing as long as you desire wholeheartedly to reach your goal of personal success! Those opportunities will be there for others to use and get ahead, but your hope is not lost because you missed them. If you change your lifestyle by investing in yourself, there will be other opportunities you will be able to use.

John Frugal and William Spendall

Remember our two friends, John Frugal and William Spendall? John did use opportunities to save money, and is using the opportunity of opportunities, himself, to reach his success. William missed many opportunities, but if he would only use this final opportunity to invest in himself, William would still be able to reach his own personal success.

You must remember that no matter how much or little time you have until retirement, if you are willing to maximize your potential savings, *you will reach success!* You need to use your own drive and desire to create the opportunity to be able to save your way to success. Take heed of the example of John and William in the previous paragraph. William would be able to save his way to success only if he would take action on his own drive and desires. It is the same with you. You must take whatever action is necessary to propel you forward to success through saving.

Sure, an opportunity is an opportunity, but if you are willing to move ahead and become a success, then it matters not what opportunities have been missed, because no matter what obstacles, challenges or failures there are, you will succeed because you know you will—because you believe in yourself. As long as you remain strong, courageous, faithful, enthusiastic and willing you will succeed. If you use your opportunity, your own mind and faith, and reach for your dreams, rather than sitting idle, waiting for them to come to you, you have as much of a chance as everyone else in succeeding! In fact, even if this is the only opportunity you use, you have as much of a chance of reaching success as the person who is many years younger! *Use your opportunity, your mind, will power, courage, strength, and abilities and success will be yours!*

Use your opportunity, yourself, by investing in yourself. Take action on your personal drive and desire to reach success. Back in chapter two, we explained that to be able to reach your savings potential and then to reach success through saving, you need to invest in yourself. We have now returned to that amazing fact. By investing in yourself, the final opportunity in the master plan of saving, you will be able to create a personal savings program. You will be able to use the method of moderation to eliminate some of the wants you have been purchasing. You will be able to increase your savings until you have reached your maximum savings potential. You will be able to reach success through saving. There is simply nothing impossible if you put your mind totally toward accomplishing what is desired. By investing in yourself, you have programmed your mind into believing you must have what you desire—and ultimately, you will get what you desire!

The Only Obstacle of Reaching Success

There is only one, and will always be only one, obstacle that can stop a person from reaching success. There may be millions of obstacles that can slow a person down, but they can all be overcome except for one. When you have completely invested in yourself, you can accomplish any goal, defeat any obstacle, and conquer any problem. There is nothing, absolutely nothing, that can stop you when you have invested in yourself. If you have the desire to obtain a goal and you are willing to completely invest in yourself to obtain that goal, you will be able to obtain it no matter what obstacles stand ready to impede your path. When you put your mind to something by investing in yourself, there is nothing you cannot do. There is only one particular obstacle that will stop your drive for reaching your goals.

The only obstacle that can stop you, is you! Yes, you are your greatest opportunity and your greatest obstacle. If you are unwilling to completely invest yourself into accomplishing the goals you want to accomplish, you simply will not be able to accomplish them. The problem is that until you have turned the desire for success into desire with enthusiasm, and are willing to discipline yourself to use your time and effort to work wholeheartedly and to gain as much knowledge as you can, you will never reach success. You will never reach any goals you want until you have disciplined yourself to invest in yourself to reach those goals.

Until you are willing to invest in yourself in order to accomplish something, you will never be able to hurdle the only obstacle that unequivocally prevents a person from reaching success. Wishing will never acquire the things you want to accomplish. Idleness will never acquire you riches. Dreaming will never bring you success. Only when you have invested in yourself by changing your lifestyle and personality to encompass the six ingredients of investing in yourself will you be able to reach any goal. Thinking hard will only give you headaches unless you are willing to take action on those thoughts. Planning, in itself, will only waste your time unless you utilize those plans. Desiring a goal will only produce disappointment unless you transmute that desire into action and accomplishment. When you meticulously and unequivocally invest in yourself you will be able to reach any and all goals you have dreamed, and any and every goal you will ever dream.

Success does not mean extreme fame or fortune. Not everyone can be a billionaire, a president of a corporation, or a movie or sports star, but everyone has the opportunity to succeed. Use your mind and faith to reach for goals that are in your grasp, not some far-flung, wild dream. You do not have to become some huge, 200-million-dollar. famous corporate giant, but *you can* become a self-reliant, happy, financially free, independent person by reaching success! You can become a truly financially independent somebody! Reach for your goals and succeed. *He who does not dream will never have a reason to succeed, and he who dreams, but never acts, will only dream about succeeding, but the man who acts on his dreams will succeed.*

Points to Ponder:

- If you are not currently working, you need to be. If you are, you need to create additional income.
- Stop buying wants to be "cool," to seek status, or to impress others; instead, make saving money and looking ahead toward your future your number one priority.
- Saving should never be stopped, or it may never be started again, and then success will never be reached. *There is never a time not to save. Every time is the right time to be saving money.*
- Many opportunities pale in comparison to the greatest opportunity of all, you. *Use your opportunity, your mind, will power, courage, strength, and abilities and success will be yours!*
- The greatest obstacle, and the only obstacle that can keep you from attaining success, is yourself. You are your only absolute obstacle. You are your greatest opportunity and your greatest obstacle.
- By investing in yourself, you remove the only obstacle that completely restrains you from reaching goals: yourself and your inability to start working towards success.

Save as much as you can, as fast as you can, and propel yourself forward to success through saving.

9
REMEMBER THE FOUR R'S:
REDUCE, REUSE, REPAIR, RECYCLE

"I recognize the right and duty of this generation to develop and use the natural resources of our land; but I do not recognize the right to waste them, or to rob, by wasteful use, the generations that come after us."

Theodore Roosevelt[1]

Reduce, reuse, repair, recycle, commonly known as the four R's of recycling, can also be used as the four R's of saving. Doing your part to help the environment gives more than you may imagine; it will also save you money.

These four words, the four R's of recycling, can save money. They may already be incorporated in your savings, without you even realizing it. In fact, these four R's have already been incorporated in *Saving Your Way to Success.*

This chapter is not about persuading you to recycle, but it is about how recycling will save you money. Some people think recycling is not necessary. If you do not think the environment is in danger, then do not do the four R's for that reason; rather, do them to save yourself money.

Reduce and Save

Reducing your waste greatly helps you to save money. Unknowingly, many people who practice the ideas behind reducing their garbage for environmental purposes are also saving. Unknowingly, many people who practice saving are probably also reducing.

Reduce and you will save. Save when you buy, and you are reducing. The two are interchangeable. Since it is requisite you use moderation to maximize your savings, it is very likely you are simultaneously reducing. If you are using moderation when you buy, you are reducing because you are buying less. Reduce how much you use and/or throw out, and you will save money. By doing one, you do the other at the same time.

The biggest money-saving technique talked about in this book is living below your means, or moderating how much you spend. Moderation is a synonym of reducing. By using moderation when you buy unnecessary things, you are also reducing. You are reducing how much you buy and reducing how much you spend.

According to Webster's 20th Century Dictionary:

Moderation: 1.The act of moderating or restraining: the act of tempering, lessening or repressing. 2. The state or quality of being moderate, or avoiding extremes; freedom from excess; temperance; restraint; reduce; to lessen in anyway, as in size, weight, amount, value, **price**, etc.; to diminish. (emphasis added)

Reduction: 1. The act of diminishing in size, dimensions, value, quantity, force, etc.; diminution, abatement; as the *reduction* of expenses. 2. Anything made or brought about by reducing, as a smaller copy, lower **price**, etc (emphasis added). 3. The amount, value, quantity, etc. by which anything is reduced or lessened; as, he made a *reduction* of five percent.[2]

Moderation and reducing both mean to lessen. By reducing how much garbage you create to save the environment, you will also save money because less garbage equals a smaller amount of money wasted. By moderating how much you buy; therefore, possibly creating less garbage, you will help the environment. It is that basic. By either reducing your garbage or moderating how much you buy, you are also probably doing the other.

You save whenever you reduce. When you reduce the amount of garbage you are throwing out, you are saving money. If you reduce the amount of packaging you buy, you reduce the amount of money you are spending. Packaging is expensive, and by reducing the amount you have to buy (such as by buying bigger containers so there is less packaging per quantity or by buying products with less plastic and packaging) you are saving. Packaging costs consist of fully one tenth of the average citizen's weekly shopping bill.[3] Think about that for a moment. If you spend $100 on average at the grocery store, $10 is automatically wasted on packaging. If you reduce how much packaging you buy, and thus throw out as garbage, you will save money.

Stop Throwing Out Your Money as "Garbage"

If you reduce the amount of trash you are putting in the garbage container, you will save money. You paid money for the things you are throwing out; therefore, by reducing how much you throw out, you will save money. Reduce, and you will save.

What is trash? According to Webster's Twentieth Century Dictionary trash is:

Any waste or worthless matter; good-for-nothing stuff; rubbish; refuse; dross; dregs.[4]

Trash is money. How can that be? If you paid for what you are throwing out as "garbage," you are throwing out the money that went to pay for what you are now throwing out. The "garbage" you throw out is actually your hard-earned money.

Trash is something you do not want. It is considered worthless stuff, of no value. The stuff you are throwing away, you believe to be worthless. The fact is, though, because you purchased what you are now throwing out as garbage, you are throwing out your hard earned money with the trash.

Is your money so worthless you are throwing it out and above that, paying the garbage collectors a hefty fee to take it away for you? The garbage may seem like only left-over food, food packaging, broken toys and old newspapers, but the fact remains, that if money was paid for whatever is being thrown out as garbage, the money paid for it is also being thrown out. Is your money so worthless you can take it out in full bags every week, leaving it on the curb for people whom you pay to take it away?

What are some items commonly thrown out? Perhaps it is a $1.50 loaf of moldy bread. Maybe the packaging on your food or other products. Or the plastic toy that broke right away. How about the seventy-five cent daily newspaper, an old pair of socks or stained shirt, or an old ripped or broken couch? There are many times when we get our money's worth out of a product. Information is extracted from the newspaper. The plastic toy may have been played with for a while. The couch could have been used for many years. You may get good use out of a product, but when you throw it out, you are still literally throwing out what you paid for it. This is why it is so important to look for value and quality when you shop.

It is amazing how much garbage is not really garbage. Unless you have a lot of money to throw away, why are you throwing it away? When you realize the garbage you despise is actually your hard-earned money, you may think twice before you throw something into the trash can. Cut back on how much you throw out—stop throwing out your money.

John Frugal and William Spendall

Let us see how our friend William Spendall throws away his money by wasting, not reducing. William, thirsty, pours himself a glass full of orange juice. Several hours go by, and he forgets about it, having only drunk half of the glass. When dinner comes, William sits down and prepares to eat. He pours himself another full glass of juice, but again only drinks half of it. He does this throughout the day, continuously forgetting about the half-full glasses. By the time bedtime rolls around William Spendall may have several half-full glasses sitting around. William has wasted juice and money without even realizing it. John Frugal, on the other hand, constantly endeavors to reduce how much he is wasting, and thus how much of his hard earned money he is throwing out.

Money can be saved when garbage is reduced. A pilot project at the Georgia Diagnostic and Classification Center in Jackson, Georgia, had inmates composting food scraps and reducing what was not used. By reducing—by not wasting food and composting rather than "garbaging" food—the Center saved money. While they used to pay $2,050 per ton of food waste that went to the landfill, the composted food scraps now save them nearly $1,800 per month.[5] By reducing how much food was wasted and thrown into the trash, they saved money.

Another reason to reduce is the garbage bill. Garbage rates continue to go up. If you still do not think of your garbage as money, then you will at least be able to descry the savings when you reduce your garbage bill. Many communities are changing from a flat rate fee to a per-amount basis. The more garbage you have, the more you pay. On the other hand, you could reduce and pay less, or eliminate and save 100%.

Plastic packaging is where a significant amount of your money is being thrown out as "garbage." Whenever you buy a product, you are also buying its packaging. When you throw out that packaging, you are throwing out money. You need to reduce the amount of packaging and plastic you buy.

- Buy bulk, or products with less packaging.
- Use a reusable bag or a box for your groceries.
- Use paper, which can easily be recycled, rather than plastic.
- Ask not to get a plastic bag when you buy only a few items at the store.
- Buy used rather than new. There should not normally be packaging with used items.

Reduce the amount of plastic and other packaging you have to buy and then throw away as "garbage," and you will be saving money.

Every year, Americans throw out 234 million metric tons of garbage—more than any other country.[6] We are a throwaway society. We live on one-use products designed and marketed to be immediately thrown out. "A society in which consumption has to be artificially stimulated in order to keep production going is a society founded on trash and waste, and such a society is a house built upon sand," wrote Dorothy L. Sayers.[7] A society based on one-use items created to only become garbage, thus a throw-away society, will not last long. When the sand sinks or shifts, the economy, based on garbage, will crumble. Just imagine how much money could be saved if only a portion of the 234 million metric tons of "garbage" was not thrown out. If the "garbage" was worth only one cent per pound, which is a very conservative guess, Americans are throwing away 4.68 billion dollars! Americans are throwing out far too much money with their trash.

Everyday, every American throws out 4.4 pounds of garbage.[8] Multiply 4.4 pounds by 365 days and you have 1,606 pounds of garbage per year per American. Stop throwing out so much money as garbage. A huge garbage burden is throwaway plates. Why spend money on those styrofoam plates just to throw them away? Sure, dishes take time to clean, but if you were only going to watch television otherwise, why throw away your hard-earned money? Use the dirty dishes and the process of cleaning them to bring the family together, or to teach the kids about work.

John Frugal and William Spendall

William Spendall is well known for the huge piles of garbage he places on the boulevard every week. Little does he realize that all of his "garbage" is actually money. Every cent he used to purchase what is now being thrown out as garbage is also being thrown out. John Frugal, on the other hand, understands that by using the four R's, especially reducing, he is able to save more money because he is reducing how much he pays for packaging, throw away products, one-use items, and garbage bills.

Are you a John Frugal or a William Spendall? Which one do you desire to be? You can increase your maximum savings potential by reducing how much of your money you are throwing out as "garbage."

Reduce the amount of food you buy if you cannot eat it and are forced to throw it out. Reduce the amount of packaging you buy, which adds a good chunk of money to the product you buy. Buy bulk, buy products with less packing, and buy less plastic. Use reusable products. All these reducing ideas will save you money.

Reuse and Save

All four R's of recycling are interrelated. So are the four R's with saving—multiplying the reward for your efforts.

Reuse and reduce are very interrelated. When you reuse a product, the product is not being thrown out. If it is not being thrown out, you are reducing the amount you do throw out.

By reusing something once, you can save enormous amounts of money. Using a product twice rather than buying it twice saves you 50%! If the product costs a dollar, two would cost two dollars. By using the product twice, you save the price on the second purchase. Saving one dollar of two dollars saves you 50%. Use your imagination to find how you can reuse what you buy. Contemplate what is constantly thrown out, then find what you always have to purchase, and then put them together. If you are always buying plastic, use the plastic you are already buying as packaging. Use your creative mind to come up with thousands of ways to reuse what you already buy, rather than buying it twice and then throwing it out after only one use.

Reuse more and save more. When you reuse something, you are saving in two ways.

1. You are saving because when you reuse something, you are doubling the value of the product.
2. By reusing a product, you reduce how much of the same product you have to buy, thus saving more money.

Yes, when you reuse a product, you are doubling its value. If the product purchased for one dollar with the recommendation of only one use is reused somehow, you double its value. Each use only costs .50$ rather than $1 per product recommended for only one use. Rather than buy two products and use each once, at a total cost of $2, you double the value of the one product that you use twice. Each use considered worth $1, doubles the products value; therefore, you got a $2 use out of a $1 product. You are getting more product for your money and you are reducing how much you spend. You save twice by reducing how much you buy and by doubling a product's value. Rather than tossing out money as worthless, or as many people say, "take out the trash," you are saving money when you reuse a product.

You reuse a product when you keep it out of the garbage by finding another use for it. By using it beyond its advertised life, or finding another use for it, you keep it out of the garbage.

Reusing saves money in a sense in which the savings may not seems obvious. You do not actually see the savings as you do the price tag. When you use a coupon or buy on sale you can quickly see your savings, but when you reuse something, there is no coupon or savings special advertisement for you to see, but this does not mean that the savings is not there.

When you reuse something, you increase the value of the money you paid for the product. If you continue to reuse a product, you will never have to buy a new one. You save by reducing how much you buy, and by reducing how much you throw out.

Repair and Save

Fixing something is one way to reuse a product. Learning how to do things yourself is a good money-saving technique discussed many times in "Saving You Way to Success." Doing it yourself saves you from expensive repair bills. For example by learning how to do basic car repair, you will save yourself money. You could save so much money from eliminating bills with the R of repair.

What can you learn to repair? There are many items you use everyday that you can learn to repair and maintain to reduce costly expenditures:

- Automobile
- Vacuum cleaner
- Bicycle
- House
- Furniture
- Radio
- Lawnmower
- Toilet
- Small appliances

By repairing, you can save a lot of money and time—and reduce waste. When you remodel your own house, you save money and time. The bills you could get from contractors by hiring rather than doing it yourself can consume a small fortune. Do not take the car to the shop; instead, repair it yourself. Do not buy a new toilet because the seat is cracked. Repair or replace the seat. Do it yourself—repair it.

This savings method does so much more than just save money. If the time comes when you cannot get someone else to help, maybe it's a holiday, or worse, you're stuck in a storm, and you do not know how to fix your car, you will be in a very serious situation. Because you cannot get it going yourself, you may have created a perilous situation as you wait out the storm. Learning to do it yourself saves you from those situations. Learning how to repair things yourself will have many benefits.

What happens when the furnace shuts down over the holidays? What if the toilet breaks down? You cannot call the repairman, because he is with his family, and you have a house full of people who have been stuffing themselves with holiday food and drink, and your toilet is not working! You are going to end up with a plugged toilet and an empty house unless you can fix it. By learning basic do-it yourself, you may be able to save yourself from such embarrassing situations that could come up, radically altering the holiday spirit of your company. Learn basic do-it-yourself and eliminate embarrassing situations.

By doing things yourself, whether it is repair, remodeling, or maintenance, you will save money. It may take time to complete the project, but the savings are enormous and far outweigh the time. Think of it as if you were the repairman to be paid. Rather than handing out $30 to $40 an hour to the repair shop, you pocket the $30 to $40 an hour by doing it yourself.

Repair things to save yourself more money. Whenever you fix, maintain or repair a product you are prolonging the life of the product. If you increase the life of a product, you get more use from your purchase. When you increase a product's life, you also reduce the amount of your garbage because you saved the product from your garbage and the landfill. Repair will not only help the environment, but it will also save.

Become a Do-It-Yourself Mechanic

Learning how to do-it-yourself is always an excellent money saver. With automobiles, this is especially true. Take the time to learn mechanics and even auto body work if it interests you. The savings from being able to repair an automobile, mechanically and appearance-wise, will be enormous—so enormous that financial commentator Jonathan Pond found that people can save $400,000 to $450,000 over 40 years as long as they hold on to their cars for at least ten years! Pond also reported that an older car's higher maintenance made no difference in the savings.[4] You will be able to save enormous money and take pride in a repair and restoration job well done. You will have a nice looking automobile, and it will be better than the spendthrift's who knows only how to drive. When his breaks down, *you* will still be cruising along.

After buying a used car, it is best for anybody to learn basic maintenance and repair. Even though it is still cheaper to buy a used automobile than a new automobile, the repair bills, will devour a good sum of your savings (though it will devour less than car payments on a new car would devour) if you do not know some do-it-yourself mechanics. Take the small amount of time to learn basic mechanics and maintenance. Knowing basic automobile mechanics and maintenance is invaluable to any automobile owner.

How I Did It

When I was a teenager, I turned the money-saving technique of restoring a used car into a valuable money-saving reality.

I was like any other normal teenager in my dream of having a nice looking hot rod. The key difference was that I restored an old car, rather than spending several times more on a new or fairly new car. I completely restored an Oldsmobile Cutlass Supreme, transforming it from a rusted, ugly vehicle, into a beautiful, powerful driving machine I was proud to drive and own. It took me several years to finally finish, but in the end, I was more proud and received many more compliments than the many other teenagers who just go out to an auto lot and purchase an expensive automobile.

Restoring a car requires time, knowledge, and money. I was able to conquer every one of these obstacles. Time was the simplest. Instead of going to a game, or going to a party, I would use some of that time to work on my restoration project. It took me longer than normal to finish my restoration project because when I first started, I knew nothing about auto bodywork, and little about mechanics. I overcame this deficiency by obtaining help from any and every source available, including family and friends, books from the library, and even occasional stops into local body repair shops and supply stores to ask questions.

Money was the most difficult obstacle. I had learned from my new knowledge about restoring automobiles that the price tag can become high and I wanted to find methods that would help me keep my costs low. Fortunately, I happened to find a gentleman who had years of prior experience in auto body work and who was looking for a job. At drastically reduced costs compared to an actual auto body repair shop, I was able to learn valuable information, and nearly finish my project in a couple months. I had another opportunity, through friends, of meeting a partially retired woman who was an excellent seamstress. She reupholstered my car seats for half the normal price. When I needed to weld new floor panels and a new rear quarter panel, an auto repair shop owner/operator helped me after hours, reducing my cost for the welding drastically. When the car was ready for paint, the final phase of the restoration, I was able to save over 50% by utilizing the services of an auto body repairman in a smaller community. He was still as much of a professional as the shops in the big city and did as good a job—maybe even better.

I used several other key money saving methods throughout the project:

- I did most of the work myself, and if I could not, I helped the person who did the work as much as I could.
- I painted the inside door trim and dash board myself.
- I gave the engine a tune-up.
- I undercoated the car myself.
- I replaced a front quarter panel myself.
- I never hired any professional at regular rates (which are very expensive), except the painter.
- Rather than buying impulsively, I compared prices, ranging from body filler and auto body tools, to a new quarter panel, to taking parts off other similar models that were not drivable.

When the project was finished, I had spent considerably less money than what might have been expected, yet my car was worth considerably more than what was spent on it.

Every car owner who wants to save money on automobiles should learn basic do-it-yourself mechanics. Do not buy a new car and spend all your money on your transportation. Unless you are already rich, successful and financially set, you should not be buying a brand new model. Instead, you should be learning basic automobile mechanics and driving a used, yet mechanically good automobile. Say a new car costs around twenty thousand dollars (a conservative estimate). Compare that price to a used car that only costs three to five thousand dollars. You might even be able to find, if you shop around, a used, older model, in good mechanical shape for less than one thousand dollars! The used car may have repairs that will come up, but the repairs would have to be over fifteen thousand dollars in order for the older vehicle to become a poorer deal than the new automobile. Even if you drive the car for fifty years, that will not happen!

How I Did It

After I had completed my restoration project, I certainly did not want it to be the car I drove around daily and to everything. Instead, I bought a car, nearly perfect mechanically, for only $100! Yes, you read it right. I bought a mechanically good driving car for $100! The front end was damaged, so it did not look nice, but the previous owner was a very knowledgeable do-it-yourselfer. In my first year of driving this car, the only repairs, excluding maintenance (oil changes, tire, fluids, air filter, etc.) were a $32 starter and a $25 set of wheel bearings I replaced myself! I saved tremendous amounts of money with this vehicle, possibly the same amounts you could be saving by buying a used car and doing the repair work yourself.

John Frugal and William Spendall

Let us look at an example of the two friends, John Frugal and William Spendall. As you may already know, John is the individual who is investing in himself to reach success through saving. William also wants to reach success; but, unlike John, he does not invest in himself to maximize his savings. William believes more in luck than in himself. John once again has shown his ability to help him increase his maximum savings, this time using do-it-yourself mechanics. His savings are enormous. He uses the do-it-yourself method on his automobile, his home, his home appliances, and anything else he knows how to repair.

John never takes big chances including trying to do a job he does not know how to do. When he is unable to fix the car, he takes it to an auto repair shop, but he makes sure to find out if he is able to learn how to fix this particular problem so the next time it happens, he will be able to do-it-himself.

William, on the other hand, thinks he is saving money when he shops around to find the best price on the repair. Little does he know that when he goes to an unfamiliar shop he does not know what type of craftsmanship will be performed. Will the repair last? Will the bill be accurate? Will the shop add unnecessary repairs to the total cost? Will the old part be used when the bill states new or remanufactured? William does not realize that he could eliminate most of this headache by going to shops he regularly uses because of good work and fair prices—but he can also eliminate it by learning how to do some of the repairs himself.

Learning auto mechanics will save you lots of time and money. If your car stalls out, breaks down, or does not even start, you may know what to do. What if you are stranded where there is no tow truck or service station or even a neighbor to change your tire or start your car? If you do not have a clue why the automobile is not working or how to find and fix the problem, then you are stranded—but if you took the time to learn some mechanics you may be able to get yourself out of this situation.

I firmly recommend that any automobile owner learn basic mechanics. It does not matter whether it is a new car, or a newer used car or even an old rusted out junk heap. This is one money saving technique that will work for anyone.

Recycle and Save

The last of the four R's is recycling: reprocessing a product to produce a new product. Recycling does the most to help the environment. It is a very beneficial means to reduce waste. It may be the last R, but it is still important.

Recycling can also save you money. When you take your recyclables to a recycling center—being paid for bringing in the recyclables—you make money and save money.

Why not take those recyclables in to earn some money rather than just throw them out as if they were worthless? They are not worthless. Take those recyclables in to earn some money rather than paying someone else to take them away as garbage. Right now only aluminum cans earn a countable amount of money when you take them to the recycling center, but as more and more recycled products are bought at the stores, the demand for recyclable products will increase; therefore, your recyclables will become worth more. Start buying recycled products to prove there is a demand for them in the marketplace, and over time, you will increase the value of your recyclables.

Taking recyclables to a recycling center may earn you some money, but that is not where the most money saved with recycling can be. You can save the most money from reducing your garbage. By recycling you are not throwing everything into the garbage, thus you are reducing. Through that process, you can save the most by recycling.

The four R's are the essence of recycling. They reduce the waste streams. They reuse products. They prolong the life of products. They reprocess and recycle valuable commodities. They do much for the environment.

The four R's are also an essence of saving. You have read how it is possible. The ways are numerous. Many people do not believe in helping the environment because they do not believe it is in danger; but they are doing just that if they are saving. By doing one, you do the other. By recycling you save money. The four R's do help save money.

Start using these four R's to save yourself money. The four R's incorporate several great methods of saving—including moderation and do-it-yourself. Begin now if you are not already doing the four R's. You will be doing two things at once by doing the four R's—helping the environment and saving money. Begin now and start reaping the rewards.

Points to Ponder:

- The four R's of recycling—reduce, reuse, repair, and recycle—will save enormous amounts of money, even though many times they are not considered money-saving techniques.
- Reduce the packaging you buy: Buy in bulk. Buy at farmer's markets. Grow your own organic garden. Buy only what you need. Use a reusable bag or box when you grocery shop. Reduce your packaging expenditure and you will save money.
- Reduce how much money you are throwing out as "garbage." Remember, everything you throw out had a purchase price, and whatever you paid for it, your money is now being thrown out.
- Save money by repairing rather than throwing something out.
- Learn how to do small household repair jobs.
- Learn how to do maintenance and small repair on your own automobile, including changing your own oil and then recycling your used oil and oil filter safely.
- Use your imagination to discover ways to reuse things you have bought. For example, use plastic bags you get as packaging, rather than going out and buying more bags or plastic wrap for your food.
- All four R's are all related, and the most related are recycling and reducing. By recycling, you are reducing how much money you are throwing out as "garbage."

The fact endures if money is paid for whatever is being thrown out as garbage, the money paid for it is also being thrown out.

10
TIME IS MONEY

"Remember that time is money,"

Benjamin Franklin.[1]

Always, always follow Benjamin Franklin's advice because time (along with effort) is one of the ingredients of investing in yourself in order to reach your goals. Use your time wisely, because it is worth money. Every passed hour is another hour lost forever. *Waste your time, and you waste the time of your life.*

Time is money—very, very valuable. With time, you can do anything. With time, you can make a substantial amount of money. Waste your time and you will not. If you waste time, you are wasting money.

The best part of time is that it is always valuable and always available to everyone. Time is very valuable and does not rely on anyone or anything to make it valuable; but you can make it more valuable by using it wisely. One person may use the valuable commodity that costs nothing, while another person may waste it. Time is always valuable, no matter what a person does with it. If you waste time, you lose it forever; use it wisely, and you gain. If you do not use it wisely, you are losing a great advantage. If you do not use time to its fullest, you waste the most valuable commodity on earth.

Time Is Very Valuable

Time is the most valuable commodity there is. It is more valuable than $100 bills, diamonds, oil, silver or even gold, because without time you cannot acquire these other things. Time may not be substantive or hold form (other than on a clock), but that does not take away from its value. It is valuable because when you use it wisely, you can become whatever you desire to be. Without time, you can not become anything. The amazing thing is, although time is the most valuable commodity on earth, it is free to all who want to use it. Time costs nothing. You do not have to use capital to purchase it and then hope it goes up in value. It costs nothing, takes nothing to acquire it and it is free. Time is *the* bargain of a lifetime.

How can time be the best investment there is? Simply because it is free and with it anything can be accomplished. You will not succeed unless you valiantly use your time wisely and ultimately move far enough ahead to consider yourself successful. When you use time wisely—a valued commodity— anything is achievable. Sure, some people are born rich, or win the lottery; but even for these people, time is the best commodity they could ever use. You do not have to buy the investment, time, but you do have to use it wisely. Use time wisely and you will be able to enjoy a financially independent, successful life.

You will not become successful unless you use your time wisely to start working towards success. No one would ever accomplish anything if they did not use their time to their advantage. When you use your time constructively, you are moving a step forward toward reaching your goals in life. If you do not use your time constructively, you will be falling back because you will lose some of your portion of time. When you generate the time to do something, by removing the wasteful time consumers that do nothing to aid in achieving your desires, you will be able to accomplish your goals. When you use time constructively, you take the most necessary step to reach your goals. Time is the force allowing you to be able to do things that over time will create success in your life.

Every person's day has only 24 hours in it. Rich people get no extra time. Politicians and popular businessmen, movie idols and sports stars get no added benefit from time. They all have the same amount of time as you do. *Time is the great equalizer; it cannot be stored away or bought for any amount of money.* Everyone needs time to reach success, and everyone gets the same amount of time in a day. It is truly the great equalizer when driving toward success.

Why then do people say things like, "I do not have enough time," or, "How does that man find the time to do those things?" or "The rich always have more time?" Everyone has the same 24 hours in a day. It only matters how you choose to use your time. Use time wisely, and you will always have enough time. When you use your time unwisely, it begins to seem you do not have any time at all. Everyone receives the same amount of time. The difference between people is the people who have control of their lives and the people who haphazardly let things happen. One uses time and becomes successful and independent, the other gets nowhere in life and dies poor. You need to use your time wisely on important goal-reaching projects, not on irrelevant time wasters. Everyone gets the same amount of time; it only matters how *you* use *your* time.

Use Time Wisely—You Only Get One Chance

The person who achieves his or her goals is the person who uses time wisely. This is a powerful fact of life. Remember it well. If you desire to succeed in life, you must be organized and use your time wisely. Do not waste your time on frivolous activities, such as watching television. If you do not use your time on projects that enrich your life and your savings account, your chances for financial success are slim to none. Use your time wisely, believe in yourself, read about and study the lives of successful people, and you will reach your goals.

A person who wastes time is the person who thinks he does not have enough time to do important things, such as working toward success, because he wastes time on things like watching television. Watching too much television turns you into a couch potato and a passive thinker. The inability to think comes from not exercising the mind or laziness. Stop using time as an excuse for not doing something. You have the time to do what you keep putting off; you just need to prioritize what you want to do, and get it done. Wasting time must be more important than making money if that is what you do with most of your time. Stop wasting time—the valuable, free time that could be used to work toward success, or even to clean out the garage or read a book—and you will see your life become more fulfilling and satisfying because things will be accomplished.

How many times have you said, "I do not have enough time?" Maybe you have said it today or this week. What this statement really means is that you have decided there is something else, more important that needs to be done. When you say you do not have enough time to do something constructive, yet are spending some of your time watching television, you are saying the television is more important than doing something constructive. You need to begin to organize your schedule and prioritize what is most and least important in your life in order for you to "have enough time."

Some people who are great time organizers still wish they could do more in a day, but these are not the same people believe they do not have enough time. These people prioritize what is most important in their day, week or month. Rather than trying to get everything done, or wasting time by not getting anything done, they succeed by prioritizing what can and should be done to become successful. These people use their time wisely, as it is supposed to be used. These people realize time is a very valuable commodity. They know that when they use their time to move a step ahead, even if it is a very small step, they are moving closer to success and are moving ahead of the people who "do not have enough time."

The lazy person is the person who wastes time; therefore, he who is also the person who thinks he does not have enough time. The problem is, though, that lazy people receive the same amount of time as everyone else. The person who is successful received the same amount of time as the person who is not successful. The person who is moving closer to success has the same 24-hour day as the person who is not moving toward success. There will always be days when you are working toward success and will wish you had been able to do more in a certain day, or wish you had used your time more wisely. The best part of this is that as you are working toward success, you will learn from your past and do what is best for your future. The person working toward success will never say, "I do not have enough time;" rather, you will ask, "How could I have used my time more constructively?"

How do you use your time? Consider that on average, Americans each week waste...

- 4 hours cleaning toilets and other household chores.
- 2 hours picking up dry cleaning and other errands.
- 51 minutes spent stuck in traffic jams.
- 24 minutes standing in lines.
- 23 minutes on hold waiting for someone to pick up the phone.[2]

Use Time to Your Advantage

The more time you use, the more money you save. Use your time wisely to earn more money and save more money. Rather than waste time, use your time to repair the automobile, clip coupons or do some other money-saving technique.

Just think: If you would acquire a part-time job, work an extra 10 to 15 hours a week and bring home an extra $90 per week, you could squirrel away an extra $4,680 in a year's time. This is what we mean by using your time constructively to reach for success.

Today's people spend too much of their time on wasteful things. The average American has 41 hours of leisure time every week, according to a study of working Americans. Of those 41 hours of free time per week, 30%—more time than on anything else—was spent watching television.[3] And then people wonder why they do not have enough time.

"More free time means more time to waste," Robert Hutchins said.[4] Having more free time should not mean more time to watch television, but it usually does. Rather than simply throwing your extra free time away by wasting it on television or some other unproductive thing, use it constructively. More free time should not mean there is now more time to waste. It should mean that there is more time to be used to earn more money, save more money and work on reaching your goals. Use all of your free time to earn more and save more. Use it to reach your goals. Use it to become a success.

How I Did It

Instead of using my spare time to watch television, I wrote, *Saving Your Way to Success*. Yes, that is right. Rather than waste my precious spare time, I passionately desired to use my time wisely. Rather than waste *my* portion of the most valuable commodity on Earth, time, I used it to develop and fine tune a savings program that I know will help you reach your financial goals. I took the time to do hours upon hours of careful research, diligent fact-finding venturing and continuous studying to create and fine tune a savings program that worked for not only me, but anyone else, including yourself.

What can you accomplish with your spare time?

Most people who complain and claim they do not have enough time are couch potatoes or some other wasteful-time users. The fact is, everyone has the same amount of minutes in an hour, hours in a day, and days in a week, some just use their time more wisely than others. If you are a person who thinks you do not have enough time, look at how you use your time. Eliminate time wasters and use your time on what you really desire to accomplish. Use your wasted time on things you have been stating you do not have the time to do. Those who complain they do not have enough time do have the time, they just need to get off the couch and do what they desire to do. "While time is important, the control of time is more important, and the effective control of time is most important," wrote George M. Bowman.[5]

Start Using Your Time Wisely

Thirty percent of 41 leisure hours is a large sum to be wasted. Think of what you could do to reach your goals in that huge amount of time every week rather than watching television. This does not mean you have to give up your leisure activities, but it does mean you need to stop wasting time. If you want to do something, do it by starting to use your time wisely. With an average of 41 hours of leisure time per American, we Americans could be accomplishing so much more. *You* could be accomplishing so much more. Forget the television or whatever it may be wasting your valuable time and do something worthwhile. Stop wasting your time and start reaching your goals.

What should you be using your spare time to accomplish?

- Learning how to save money.
- Learning how to spend your money wisely.
- Learning how to invest money.
- Learning how to become well informed with your personal finance.
- Learning how to become financially independent.

John Frugal and William Spendall

John Frugal and William Spendall simultaneously came upon an offer to earn extra income through a sideline business. William, rather than acting immediately, wrote down the necessary information, then went shopping. Afterward, he went home to watch his favorite television program. He decided he would think about the offer tomorrow. John, on the other hand, went immediately home to contemplate whether the offer was valid and if it was a possibility for him. After deciding he wanted to try it, John acted on it the same day. John used time to his advantage to get the business before William, who did not use his time wisely.

What do you use your time on? Do you procrastinate? Or are you like John Frugal who takes action on new found opportunities? Have you ever been like William Spendall and sat idle as opportunities passed you by? Become a John Frugal and start using your time wisely.

Although time is free, it can create an awesome advantage for people who use it properly, compared to people who haphazardly use it to accomplish something. The people who use time to their advantage are the people who will reach success.

Television Is an Enormous Time Waster

Watching television is one of the biggest leisure activities Americans do, and is also one of the biggest time wasters in this country. There is absolutely no reason you cannot relax every once and a while, but when the television becomes the essence of your life, then it has become an impediment to success. Are you finding yourself recording your favorite shows for fear you might miss an episode? Do you frequently record one program while watching another? Do you occasionally or frequently plan your day, evening or weekend around programs you want to watch? Are there just some programs you cannot possibly miss? If any of your answers are an affirmative, television has become an impediment in your drive for success.

Stop being a coach potato if you are one. Whether or not you are a coach potato, I recommend unplugging the television for a week (the 4th week of April is Official Turn the TV off week). This simple step will be a true test of willpower and will clearly show if you control the television or if the television controls you. This experiment will prove many things about what the priorities in your life are.

You may be thinking, "That's impossible!" The fact is, it is only as impossible as you make it. By turning off the television, you will prove to yourself what is valuable to you. If you cannot resist, and before the seventh day is over, the television is back on, you will know the television controls you. By giving in during the week, or by not even trying the experiment, you will have proven to yourself that television does control your life, and you do not care if you waste a lot of time watching it. Think about this: You have an inanimate object in your living room controlling your life!

This is the ultimate test of television and its role in your life. Conquer it and find for yourself a new path to success. Fail it and fail yourself and your chance of success. Eliminating the television for one week should be easy. Use the radio to catch the news and weather, and you will be fine. Eliminate the television for one week and watch what you can accomplish with your time.

During this week, make a precise list of everything you do. Post it somewhere in your home—maybe on the refrigerator—where you can see it. You may want to title it, "The Things I Did the Week I Did not Watch TV." This will be your personal reminder of how much you *can* get done with the television turned off.

Use the week of no television to bring the family together. Television gets in the way of too many families. With the television off, concentration will go to other important things such as your children's schooling and future. With less time wasted, more time will go to useful things producing constructive results. Have you not told your children at some time or another, "Turn that TV off!"? This experiment will bring the family together if everyone attempts it. If the family relationship does not improve significantly, examine the experiment to see if there were other results. Maybe it did not work for your family. Maybe it helped in some other way. Maybe it needed more compliance from family members to make it a successful experiment. Even if it accomplished little, it should at least have brought attention to who, what, and why the family is the way it is. Stop watching TV and start watching your family instead.

No television for a full week is a very valuable experiment. Think of how much you can accomplish with all your time used to watch television. Visualize in your mind everything you want and can accomplish in this experimental week and then do it! You may be surprised at what you will get done with the television off. After the week is over, sit back, relax and enjoy a good program, but always remember what the experiment accomplished and taught you and your family.

Television is not the only thing time is wasted on, but it is the biggest. More time is wasted on television than on anything else because it hooks, manipulates, and addicts people. Yes, sometimes, television programs can be beneficial, but when the television comes on in the morning and stays on until bedtime, it has become a time-wasting addiction. Other things can waste time, but watching too much television is the biggest time waster that there is.

Children and Television Are Not a Good Mix

Who watches the most television? Children do. By the time today's children reach the age of 70, they will have watched 7 to 10 years of television.[6]Seven to ten years of their life wasted on watching too much television! Children are the biggest viewers of television and thus are the biggest wasters of time on television. Children waste too much time on watching television when they should be using their imaginations.

On Tuesday, December 16, 1997, 594 children were taken to the hospital for watching television! Nearly 600 people, aged 3 to 20, suffered spasms about 20 minutes into the popular cartoon "Pokemon" Japanese for "little monsters."[7] Which scene sickened the viewers? TV Tokyo did not say. News reports blamed it on a strobe light flashing of the eyes of a character and an explosion that lasted several seconds on the program. Both received the blame for the viewers suffering epilepsy-like symptoms. As of the following morning, 111 people were still in the hospital. This is just one instance of what television can do to a person, especially children.

Help with your child's future and teach your child to watch less television. Cut back on how many hours your children watch. You may be saving them years of their lives. Rather than have so many wasted years, they will have some of those extra years free to move toward their goals. Everyone may have the same amount of time, but children who learn to watch less television will have more time to reach their goals—giving them an advantage.

One of the worst things happening in too many homes today is the use of the television as a babysitter. It may help for one day or evening, but it is destroying your children's future. What are your children getting from those cartoons? Are your children learning anything purposeful? Would not it be better for them to use their creativity and play with toys or friends? Maybe your children could read a book or learn about saving money. If you are using the television as a substitute for babysitting your own children, stop! You could be ruining a part of your children's future!

Too Much Socializing Can Ruin Your Savings Plan

Socializing is fun, exciting and occasionally can be very rewarding, but have you ever kept track of how much money is spent on one social event? You would probably be surprised at how much money and time is devoured. What then happens when one social event turns into dozens upon dozens of social events? Socializing begins to deter you from your goal of financial freedom.

When expensive socializing becomes excessive, the benefits may or may not still be there, but the negative consequences will be. Excessive socializing will mean excessive spending, loss of a lot of precious time and little saving. Socializing can become like a hungry monster devouring your money and time.

Like television, socializing in itself is not a time waster. Only when it changes your lifestyle does it become a time waster. Do you sometimes put off important jobs because you are going to a social event? Has socializing become repetitious? Do you see less of your family because you are spending a lot of time at social events for work? Is socializing becoming a status symbol? An affirmative to any of these questions could suggest socializing has become a time waster impeding your drive for success. Too much socializing is too much of a good thing and will only hinder rather than help.

Wasted time is a lost commodity. Why then do so many people socialize so much? It is because they are status seekers. Status seekers may have enormous incomes and expensive "things", but they will never be successful until they start using some of their social time to create a personal savings program and then follow it. Socializing and status seeking will never help you reach success, which is a true status symbol, if that is what you desire.

Use Your Time Wisely

Which category of people do you fit into? People who waste time, or people who use time wisely? The people who waste time are the people who will never reach true success. They will never have independence or financial freedom, because they lack the ambition to work their way out of their position to a higher standard of saving and success. The people who become successful are the people who use their time to reach goals and accomplish objectives. To use time constructively means to step a little bit closer each day to reaching your goals. When you use time wisely, success recompenses you for the sacrifice of your "free" time. Use your time wisely, and happiness, financial freedom, self-reliance, peace of mind and complete independence will be your reward.

Without time, you can do nothing else. With time, you can do anything. William Spendall spends the hour watching television. John Frugal spends the time making and saving money and becoming a success. Both John and William had the same hour, but William wasted it. Understanding how powerful and valuable time is, John Frugal used the hour to make and save money and to come one step closer to his goal of success.

If you use your time wisely, you will get ahead of the person who wastes time. If you are not wasting time, you are using time wisely, which could be saving you enormous amounts of money. Maybe the saving effects, not seen immediately, will be there even if never seen at all. Rather than waste time, use it to cut coupons, learn about saving, work on your savings program, reuse a product or repair something. Use time wisely to save rather than wasting the time and money. Do it yourself rather than paying out expensive repair bills with the excuse of paying those bills to free up your time to do other things, including just sitting at home watching television. Use your time to save yourself money.

One reason time is so extremely valuable is because you can use it wisely to work on your savings program. Use time wisely to engineer, experiment, adapt, and perfect your savings program. Use time wisely to calculate your potential and actual savings. Use time wisely to create a list of goals and dreams and what and how successful you want to be. Use time wisely, and success will be yours.

"I hope you employ your whole time, which few people do... a thing so precious as time, and so irrecoverable when lost," wrote Lord Chesterfield, an English statesman.[7] Stop wasting the time of your life, and start employing your whole time advancing your goals. You will not be able to recover lost time, but you can begin to capture the value of time yet to come if you begin now. Use *your* time to help *you* reach *your* savings potential.

Points to Ponder:

- If you waste time, you waste the most valuable commodity on earth.
- Without time, a person can do nothing, and yet every single person receives the same amount of time.
- Time is the great equalizer; it cannot be stored away or bought for any amount of money.
- By using time wisely, you will be able to earn and save more money.
- Television is the biggest waster of time. Follow the test of no television for a week to ascertain if you control the television, or if it controls you.
- The biggest audience of television with the most negative consequences is children. The habits they form when they are young will probably stay with them for the rest of their lives. Many years will become wasted unless you, as a parent, help reduce your children's television watching when they are young.
- Another enormous time waster is socializing. Going to parties, receptions and other events is fun, but when it becomes excessive, it becomes a major impediment in your drive for success.
- When used wisely, time can become an advantage. Like John Frugal and William Spendall, we are classified into two categories: people who use time wisely and accomplish goals or people who waste time and will never become a success.

Waste your time and you waste the time of your life.

11
EARN MONEY THROUGH SAVING

"A penny saved is a penny earned."

Benjamin Franklin[1]

Franklin's quote is the most basic element and the best reason to save. Most people do not understand how saving can be earning. They have been taught that only working can bring about earning. This is simply not true. As Benjamin Franklin clearly understood, earning can also come from saving.

How can you earn from saving? As you have been able to discern, our two friends, John Frugal and William Spendall, both hope for success, but John is probably the only one who is going to reach success. William will not reach success, because he is a spendthrift, has not invested in himself and has not used the many money-saving methods John uses. William saves only haphazardly, does not want to devote too much of his "precious" time and does not like to work hard day in and day out—like John does. John has invested in himself, has created a personal savings program and an account record book, has maximized his savings potential and uses his time and effort to save money with every opportunity he can. John also knows that by starting as soon as possible, and by continuous saving, his small savings account will grow exponentially. He knows that by saving he can also earn more money, which in turn he can then save, which in turn will earn him more money. It is a full circle continuously compounding as his money makes more money for him. You can earn more money because you save money!

Examine the following illustration. It is a clear picture of the full circle of saving is earning. If you save your money, you earn more money. If you save that earned money, you will once again earn more. It is a full circle, never stopping, and always building your wealth for you.

Money Saved = Money Earned = Money Saved = Money Earned = Money Earned =

The Full Circle of Saving is Earning

John Frugal and William Spendall

William Spendall has earned $50 so far today, but has a chance to earn another $20. Since he is a hard worker and wants to work longer to make more, he takes the opportunity. He now has $70—but pays the car repair bill of $30 and has $40 dollars left.

John Frugal also has $50, but does not take the opportunity to work extra and earn extra money. If this seems odd, it is because John is working smarter. Instead of the extra work, John fixes his car. By fixing the car, John is saving $30 that would have gone to the car repair shop. He still has $50 dollars—$10 more than William does. John has worked less but earned more. John has earned by saving.

By saving rather than earning, you can end up with more money. It is better to save $30 than earn $20 in the same amount of time. You can have more money by saving more money.

The Reason to Save Is the Reason to Succeed

You can earn from saving, which in turn, allows you to be able to reach success through saving. This is the ultimate reason to save. There are many reasons to save, such as to climb out of debt, to have a secure financial foundation and to prepare for the future, but they all need saving to earn money from saving to reach these goals. By earning through saving, saving becomes your key to success.

Earning money through saving will make success possible. Saving will get you out of debt. It will help you stop addictions or other actions causing excessive spending. It will help you reach goals. It will help you become financially independent. It will help you become successful. The incentive of being able to earn money from saving helps obtain every other recompense. "A penny saved is a penny earned" is the ultimate reason to save.

A saved dollar is an earned dollar; that is why saving can make you a success. When you save, you are earning money above conventional means—putting you a step ahead of people who are only earning money through the conventional means of working. This advantage gives you the opportunity to become a success.

The reason to save is the reason to succeed. Some people save money to be able to buy a car, some new furniture or a big home theater system. Some people save money for a rainy day. Some people save money to take a trip or some other type of vacation. Some people save money to be prepared for an anticipated expense, such as marriage, having a child or buying a home. Some people save money in case there is an unexpected expense, such as home repairs, car repairs, or maybe even another child. Some people save money because they desire to succeed in life.

Why are you saving? Why do you desire to reach your maximum savings potential? Certainly, many of the above reasons are good reasons to save money. In fact, having money to handle known and unknown future expenses is a part of having financial freedom. The main reason, though, that you should be saving is to succeed. By saving, you acquire more money—enough to allow you to become independent, financially free, self-reliant and happy, and have peace of mind for the rest of your life. The way to reach success is through saving, and the reason to save is the reason to succeed.

Earn Money by Not Spending Money

There are three methods to earn money:

- By saving
- By investing
- By working

If you know saved money can earn you money, you will get ahead more quickly and more efficiently and reach your financial goals.

How I Did It

I used the idea of saving is earning during the time when I worked toward my goal of 50% savings (see chapter two). As the caretaker of an apartment building, I was able to drastically reduce my rent payments. By doing this, I reduced my living expenses every month, and because my expenses were reduced, I was able to save more of my income. At the end of every month, I ended up with more money than if I had not had the job of caretaker. I did not earn the extra money in my pocket book through conventional methods, but I earned it through saving.

An interest-earning savings account is a basic example of how saving can earn money. This is the only conventional means by which saving earns money. Most people can only think of this method of earning money by saving, but there is another method as well.

Not spending—and thus saving—your money is the unconventional method of earning money. Think back to the example of our two friends, John Frugal and William Spendall, and their car repairs. John saved $30 while William earned $20 from working. When all was said and done, John, who earned through saving, had $10 more than William, who earned by working. Not spending money, thus saving money, will earn money.

Stop being a part of the crowd. Take a step forward to become a frontiersman on the land of earning by saving. Impress others with how much money you have even if they have a higher-paying job. You have more money because you know the secret of the unconventional method of earning money. Go forward and start saving your money so you can unconventionally earn more money.

John Frugal and William Spendall

You earn whenever you save. When you spend, you lose your dollar, but when you save, you still have your dollar. Take the example of John Frugal. Rather then spending $20 and having Jiffy Lube change his oil, John changes his own oil; he wants to save as much of his money as he can. John has $30 dollars in his pocket, but will only part with the bare minimum. John is going to buy an oil filter and five quarts of oil for $8. ($1 per quart of oil and a $3 oil filter, both on sale). John has saved $12. He has ended up with $22, rather than the $10 had he taken his car to Jiffy Lube. If it takes John only 30 minutes to change his oil, the $12 saved figures out to an hourly-earning rate of $24 per hour. Again, John has earned through saving.

Money Saved Pays High Dividends

Think of saving as an investment. The small amount of time you devote to studying and understanding, then changing for the better, how you spend and save your money, is an investment paying major dividends. When you save one hundred dollars, it is like getting a return on an investment, except it would take a lot more time and money to get a return comparable to what is gained from saving. Saving is a no-risk, extremely high return, investment—and it is tax-free! Saving is the best non-working method of earning more money.

Scott Burns, a syndicated columnist, gives an example of how saving money can actually give you a better return than investing in the stock market. A family with a grocery budget of $150 a week could save around $750 per year at the very conservative rate of about 10% savings with coupons and other money-saving methods. This would amount to a taxable equivalent income of about $1,000. Burns then went on to state that you would need to own more than $22,000 worth of shares in a major food company stock, such as General Mills, to earn that much.[2]

In his article, Burns mentions that by earning through saving, you are able to earn tax-free money. Tax-free? Yes, by saving your money you are earning money tax-free! The government cannot tax you because you are a savvy shopper who purchased an item for $5 that costs everyone else $10. At the end of the sale, you have $5 more than the person who spent $5 more. You earned $5 tax-free! You also saved on taxes because instead of having to pay taxes on a $10 purchase, you only have to pay taxes on $5. The government cannot tax earnings coming from saving money (except on interest earned on accounts). There is nothing illegal or unscrupulous about it. By saving your money, rather than spending, you earn money completely tax-free. Any other earnings—capital gains, wages, inheritances and sales—are taxed. Invest valuable time into saving through earning, and then begin receiving an enormous return on your tax-free investment.

First Learn to Save—Investing Comes Next

Investing is a great addition to getting ahead for a person who already saves a good percentage of their income, but for a person just trying to get ahead saving is the route to take. Why? Because investments can create enormous returns, but they can also create enormous losses; and saving will create enormous returns without any possibility of ever losing money. Both need information and experience to make them work, but with saving you just cannot lose money—while with investing, substantial money can be lost.

Does this make saving better than investing? Absolutely not! They each compliment each other. Investing is how you grow your money. Saving is how you have more to invest. If you do not invest and take risks, your money will not grow substantially. You will not be able to invest, though, if you are overburdened with debt and all of your money every month is swallowed up by mountains of bills.

Your saved money will not grow substantially unless you take the risk to invest a sizable portion of it. You cannot expect to become wealthy by saving only $100 a month and sticking it in a minimal interest paying savings account. You need to invest your money in investment vehicles that over the long term will grow your money substantially.

The chart, "Comparison of Stock Market Investment Growth versus Savings Account Growth," clearly illustrates why investing your money is a part of the strategy of accumulating great wealth. Compare the values of a 5% savings account growth rate versus a 10% (average yearly growth rate) stock market growth rate. If you invest $500 each per month for 30 years in both a savings account, and in the stock market, your money would have only accumulated to $418,000 in the savings account, but would have accumulated to a whopping $1,140,000 in the stock market. By earning a 10% compounded monthly growth rate versus a 5% compounded monthly growth rate, you would be able to more than double your total wealth accumulation at the end of 30 years.

If you want your money to grow, you need to take risks by investing your money. Letting your money earn minimal interest in a saving account encompasses very little risk. Investing in the stock market, real estate, starting a business or commodities *is* risky. Saving is not necessarily better than investing, but *if you have not first mastered how to save you will not have any money to invest!*

Comparison of Stock Market Investment Growth versus Savings Account Growth

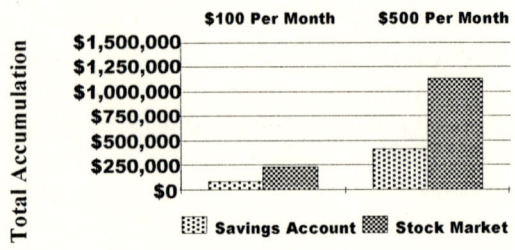

After you have created your own savings program, have reached your maximum savings potential, and have money put aside in case of an unexpected disaster or enormous expense (approximately 6 months to 1 year of income), investing is your next step in your progress for wealth and financial success. Investing helps you reach success; but if you have not learned how to save, how are you going to reduce your bills and debt so you have money to invest?

You must begin by saving first. Before you invest, you must do careful research to ensure you do not lose any of your money. With saving, you can begin immediately. Learning how to save must come before investing.

Saving Is Earning

Let us say you buy a product for one dollar normally costing two dollars. By buying used, using coupons, or any other of a multitude of methods to save, you pay less. You can now buy two of the same product with the same amount of money that normally buys only one. You have doubled the value of your money. You have not literally earned money, but you have earned it through saving.

John Frugal and William Spendall

One interesting way you can earn through saving is apartment managing. As an investment, John Frugal buys a 4-plex income rental property. John moves into one of the units to save money. William Spendall tries to explain, incorrectly, that living in one of the units will cut down on income from the property. Rather than four units, there are now only three units bringing in income. John knows better than to believe this. John is not earning literally, but is earning through saving. John is saving the rent he would normally have to pay by living in one of the four units, giving John much more money in his pocket. Think of it as John Frugal paying out the rent but getting it back into his own pocket because he owns the building. Rent, in essence, being collected on all four units is earning through saving.

We could give you many more examples. They would all produce the same concept: you can earn through saving. When you earn by saving, you are not literally earning money, but you are earning it through saving.

Having a substantial savings account—let us say $25,000, is like having another person working for you, while you are at work, continuously earning interest for you. The more you save, the more you will earn. The more of the interest earned you save, the more interest you will earn in the next interest cycle. Double your savings account to $50,000—now it is like having the person work doubly hard for you, because you will earn double the interest. Remember—your interest bearing account never sleeps. You will always be earning money from your savings account, which is working for you. Put another person to work for your success by accumulating your savings to $10,000 to $20,000, so you can earn money every moment of the year.

We have been taught work is the key to making money. It is, but saving can also earn money. To earn money, work—but to get ahead of the crowd, earn money through saving. By earning through saving, you have much more money to use to become successful. People always want more money. Saving is the best and easiest way to get the extra money. If you want more money, you should be saving. Many people do not think of saving as earning—that is why many people do not save. When more people realize and understand this concept, more people will save.

Do you want to earn more than your spendthrift neighbor does? Do it through saving. Watch how your savings account grows as the spendthrift neighbor continues to spend. The spendthrift neighbor may be buying the new cars, boats, and clothes every year, but watch the spendthrift neighbor's eyes bulge out when he goes into debt and sees you living a financially independent, successful life. Overspending by using credit cards, continuously using loans and living from paycheck to paycheck will only lead to debt and possible bankruptcy, or at least barricade even the remote possibility of moving ahead toward independence and success. Save now, and you will be driving along in the fancy car while your once spendthrift neighbor stares in awe out of the small window of the poor house.

Benjamin Franklin's quote is the ultimate reason to save. All other reasons are subordinate. Earning through saving is what helps makes saving the key to success. Most people like to earn money. Why are they not saving? They do not realize they can earn through saving.

Points to Ponder:

- By saving money, you are earning money, and by earning through saving, you have a better chance of reaching success, which is the reason to save.
- When you do not spend a dollar, you earned the dollar again, because your savings accumulation has grown by one dollar, rather than decreased.
- When you save a certain percentage of a purchase, you are receiving a return of that percentage on your money, because your pocket book now has more money in it than if you had not saved. You have earned dividends because you saved.
- You must learn both to save and to invest. However, always remember—you must first reduce your bills, or save some of your money, before you can invest some money.
- Saving is not hoarding. Saving is earning. Surpass the spendthrift neighbor with the high paying job, fancy house and luxury cars by saving your way to financial freedom.
- If you want to have money, you must have a plan to save a percentage of the income of every paycheck you earn.

The reason to save is the reason to succeed.

12
DEBT

"Rather go to bed supperless, than rise in debt."

Benjamin Franklin[1]

If you can earn through saving, why are you not saving? Alternatively, maybe the question is—can you save? Or are you in debt and forced to pay mountains of bills?

Debt is the effect of an ineffective savings program. Spend and the chances of your going into debt are good. Spend excessively to the point where it becomes an addiction and it will ultimately lead to debt. Save, and reduce the possibility of debt or maybe even eliminate the chance of debt all together. The more money saved and the longer you have been saving, or are committed to saving, the better the chance of eliminating the possibility of debt ever occurring. Good savings habits can keep you out of debt during your lifetime.

Bankruptcy: the Miscreant of Financial Freedom

Debt leads to bankruptcy. Bankruptcy is the worst economical problem that can happen to a person. Although it is possible to overcome bankruptcy, it is still very tough to rebound from it. It takes many years and lots of time, effort and sacrifice to actually get out of bankruptcy and back on the road toward success. The road of recovery from bankruptcy may be the bumpiest, longest and most barricaded economic road there is.

There is nothing as abhorrent and horrific to a person's financial life as bankruptcy. It can be, and sometimes is, the demise of a person's financial life. Bankruptcy is the miscreant of financial freedom. It is one of the biggest obstacles regarding your financial life. It can be like an impregnable barrier that cannot be hurdled, but this chapter will explain how maximizing your savings can defeat this tremendous impediment. Bankruptcy may very well be the grim reaper of financial well being, but it can be defeated.

Bankruptcy is a difficult obstacle to overcome, and an obstacle you should avoid. With bankruptcy, you have the opposite of what you will have when you become successful. Bankruptcy is the villain for anyone who desires to become financially free. How can you become financially free when you have buried yourself into debt so far that the only option left is bankruptcy? Yet you can crawl out of the hole of debt and bankruptcy. If you have already filed bankruptcy, it is time to start over, to start anew; it is time to renew your drive for success.

Bankruptcy leaves you with little in financial terms. With bankruptcy, you could lose many, if not all, of your wealth, net assets and material possessions. You could lose your house, car, savings, investments, and maybe your job. Worse than losing various assets is losing financial status. Bankruptcies always leave the impression you cannot manage your money. Your credit will plummet and take your financial life with it.

An Addiction to Spending Will Only Lead to Bankruptcy

Bankruptcy is horrible, but what causes it? Debt. What causes debt? Spending, the opposite of saving, is the culprit. Careless spending causes bankruptcy. Saving, therefore, eliminates the possibility of bankruptcy. Bankruptcy comes from unpaid bills and loans. Bankruptcy is simply spending more money than what is coming in—living beyond your means. Bankruptcy is the effect of a long period of a growing negative cash flow. There may be other apparent faults for bankruptcy, but even those would not be there if it were not for the abundance of spending. Personal bankruptcy is really the net result of poor money management and living beyond one's means.

Why do some people spend too much? It could be they are addicted to spending. Like anything else, spending can become an addiction for some people. If a person cannot quit spending, just like a person cannot quit smoking, it has become an addiction. Like an alcoholic, the person does not think he or she has an addiction, but the problems are still there. Most people never think of spending as an addiction, but it can be when it becomes excessive and causes horrible effects such as bankruptcy. People go into bankruptcy usually because they were addicted to spending and/or they had poor money management; therefore, they spent well over their income. They were living beyond their means; therefore, they had a negative cash flow for too long.

Bankruptcy is the outcome of a spending addiction. It leaves the person in economic ruins. If you are on the road toward substantial debt and eventually bankruptcy stop the addicting run on spending and start saving before it is too late.

Unlike other addictions, there is no help for the addiction of spending until you hit rock bottom. There is no AA, quit-smoking program or Gamblers Anonymous. In fact, not until you reach bottom at bankruptcy court is the problem even recognized. Bankruptcy court, as the medicine for the addiction, is in actuality the effect of the addiction. Bankruptcy is not a cure to a spending addiction. If you do not change your money habits by investing in yourself, you will never be able to jump off the revolving wheel of debt. It is up to you to stop the causes, the spending addictions, before it is too late.

Bankruptcies in the United States are increasing in a snowball effect every year. In the 12 months ended in march 2002, a record 1.5 million Americans declared personal bankruptcy–up 15.1% from the previous year.[2] This is a sharp increase from 1996, when 1.1 million Americans declared bankruptcy, which was already up 28.6% from 1995 and up 44.1% from 1994.[3] In fact, the bankruptcy rate has increased so dramatically recently that from 1992 through 1998, one out of every twenty U.S. households filed for bankruptcy.[4] That is far too many bankruptcies. They have become commonplace. Take the following steps to begin removing debt and the possibility of bankruptcy from your life:

1. If you have not already done so, begin an income and expense report.
2. Immediately cut up every credit card. You do not need one for emergencies. Leave none untouched.
3. Discipline yourself to reduce your spending and begin earning extra income by getting a part-time job above your full-time job. The only two choices to reduce debt are to spend less and earn more; but, if you do both, you double the speed in which you will eliminate your debt.
4. Develop a strategy to begin paying off your debt. Remember—doubling your minimum monthly payments on a $2,000 credit card balance will reduce the time required to pay it off from 31 years, 2 months to only 3 years![5]
5. Most importantly, stick with your new strategy to get out of debt and to become financially independent.

Resist the Temptation of the Credit Cards

The enticer, which takes most people into the pit of debt, is the credit card and its ability to give a person access to instant cash. Credit cards have benefits, but also huge, numerous bad effects. The misuse of credit cards is a big problem in our society today. Why not use credit cards? They give the availability of thousands of instant dollars at your fingertips. Then comes the statement with the enormous interest payments—the kicker of credit cards. There is no real advantage to a credit card when you roll over the debt every month. With a savings program you will have the necessary funds available to make large purchases with cash rather than pay a lot more for the product because of the added cost of interest with credit cards.

Americans have far too many credit cards. In 1994, with the inclusion of store credit cards, Americans possessed 1.1 billion credit cards—12 cards per household—equal to at least 12 types of debt in each American home on average! In the past 5 years alone, the top credit card companies, American Express, Diners, MasterCard and Visa have jumped 42% from 2.6 cards per household to 3.7.[6] In fact, we have so many credit cards that credit-card and revolving debt totals $589 billion![7] This many credit cards per American household is far too many. Stop the debt and start saving.

How I Did It

Am I a culprit? Yes, I too am a part of this seeming overabundance of credit cards. Having and using credit cards, in themselves, is not a problem. Many people use credit cards and do not go into debt. I have and use credit cards, but do not get into debt because I use them. The problem is not with the credit cards in themselves. The problem comes from the misuse of credit cards.

Many people make payments and stay below their limits—not good enough if you are still paying the interest of 16, 17, 18% or more. Why? Because you do not have the cash. If that is the reason you have credit cards, or even if it is for easy access to a sizable amount of money, you are leading yourself into the addiction of spending. A credit card is an extension of money on a per-use basis—which comes with excessive interest charges to cover the credit card company's expenses. When a credit card is used, you are stating you absolutely need the particular product even though you currently do not have the money to pay for it; but you are willing to go into debt for it and pay a lot more for it in the future so you can have it now. That is a spending addiction. Even if you do make payments, you are still in debt as long as you have an outstanding balance; you are still dangling on a wire over the abyss of bankruptcy.

You need to stop rolling over your payments every month by only paying the minimum required amount. You need to start paying off every statement when it is due, so you will not be engaged in the revolving wheel of debt. If you only pay the minimum payment, a $2,000 charged credit card would incur

$8,202 in finance charges before you pay the bill completely in 31 years and 2 months.[8]

How can you stay away from the revolving wheel of debt?

1. Reduce the amount of credit cards you have.
2. Keep a record of every purchase you make with your remaining credit cards. This way when the statement comes, you will already know what is due. You will have already set aside the necessary funds to pay the bill.
3. Although they are convenient, try valiantly not to use credit cards for emergency money situations; instead, dip into your emergency savings account.
4. Stay focused. Do not let one month's payment slip by. Always pay the full bill for every statement when it is due.

A credit card is an advance of money. You are spending money that really is not there. You hope you will make money in the future to pay the credit card, but there is no guarantee. A credit card company is loaning you money at a very high interest rate. The company is advancing you money on a loan in the same manner as a bank would were you to take out a loan. Simply stated, a credit card is a high-priced loan for things you *hope* your future income will be able to pay for.

All a credit card is based on is hope that you will be able to pay it off with future income. You are guessing what your future will bring, not planning for what you desire your future to be, when you create the habit of rolling over your credit cards payments every month. You hope you will be able to pay off the debt of the loan of other people's money. There are too many hopes and guesses and not enough certainties in credit card misuse.

With a credit card, you are spending money you do not even have yet. Spending money before you have it is the prelude of debt and bankruptcy. *That is* an addiction. When a person cannot get enough from personal earnings and has to go out and get more money from other means including credit cards and loans, then spending has become an addiction. Credit cards are a part of the addiction of spending.

There is only one proven method that will help you with your credit card spending problem—cutting up every credit card you have in your possession, and then using all your will-power to resist the temptation of acquiring any credit cards in the future. There is absolutely no other method that will help you with your credit card problem as instantaneously as this method. You may have to get a consolidation loan, or get some other type of outside help to remove the debt you have already accumulated; but, unless you are willing to get rid of *every* card you have and can resist *every* new temptation that appears, everything else you do will be to no avail. Even if you keep just one card for emergencies or some other implausible excuse, you are walking the line between pulling yourself out of your debt problem and sinking completely into the quicksand of financial ruin through bankruptcy. Resist the temptation, and you will, gradually at least, climb your way out of financial debt and into financial freedom.

Saving Is Your Escape Route from Debt

There is only one way to free yourself from the chains of debt—saving. There is no other method that will remove the debt and procure for you financial freedom so beneficially as saving does. Ann Landers, in her newspaper column, responded to a letter about a mom who was trying to help her debt-stricken daughter. Three years after turning eighteen, and after many credit cards maxed out, the daughter had accumulated a debt of $14,000! The worried mom and her husband were grievous over their daughter's situation and with a sincere heart, helped the daughter get a consolidation loan. Within the next year the daughter had accumulated yet another $9,000 in debt. In a panicked attempt to rescue the daughter from the abyss of debt and bankruptcy, the father gave the daughter an interest-free loan of $17,000. Within the next eight months, rather than reducing her debt, the daughter had accumulated yet another $5,000. Ann Lander's solution to the impending disaster was for the daughter to cut up all credit cards *now*, and for her parents to quit bailing her out, because she will never be able to learn how to deal with her finances.[9] She will never become financially independent, but would rather be a dependent for the rest of her life, unless she learns to resist the addiction she has to credit cards. Ann Lander's final recommendation was for the daughter to get help through a credit counselor who, unlike the parents, would be impervious to emotions. Get help, if you must, but the best method to progress from the abyss of debt to the light of financial freedom is with saving.

Saving is the lifeline thrown down when you are in the great abyss of debt and bankruptcy. When you invest in yourself to create a personal savings program, and stick with it, you will be able to climb out of the abyss of financial debt. Your climb may not be swift, or continuous, but it can be accomplished, no matter how gradual. As long as you invest in yourself in obeying the power of saving, you will be able to climb out of the abyss of debt. There will never be a time or an obstacle keeping you from saving your way to success. Desire success, and realize ardently there is absolutely no obstacle out there you cannot surpass, and you will be able to climb out of the abyss of debt.

Only when you give up, or do not even begin, will you be defeated. You are your greatest asset and your greatest obstacle. When you invest in yourself with desire, wholehearted work, time and effort, discipline, knowledge, and enthusiasm, you will be able to conquer any obstacle impeding your path to success. If you do not invest in yourself, if you do not create a savings plan, and if you do not start, you will never reach success. Until you desire ardently that saving will be the key to your success, you simply will not reach success through saving. Saving can and will get you out of the abyss of debt when—but only when you desire it to.

When you are not in debt, you may not have the nicest things, but they will be paid for. You may have rough times, but if the debts come due, and there are no funds to pay them, the times will be even worse. When you are in debt, your whole life begins to rotate around the debt. Forced to think about debt and do nothing else, you are controlled by the debt. "A man in debt is so far a slave," Ralph Waldo Emerson stated.[10] Do not become a slave to debt and spending. Become free and successful with saving.

Points to Ponder:

- You may not have the nicest things after defeating debt, but they will be paid for, and you will be able to move forward to success.
- Bankruptcy is one of the biggest obstacles of reaching success. Spending, thus not saving, is the seed growing into debt and bankruptcy. Spending beyond your means is like taking ten steps back in your process for financial freedom.
- Steps to eliminate debt:

1. Increase your earning potential. If necessary, start a part-time job above your full-time job to increase your income.
2. Do not use credit cards. If you have credit cards, cut them up immediately.
3. Discipline yourself to reduce your expenditures.
4. Establish a savings account early in life.
5. Spend wisely. Create a personal savings program to aid you in your quest.
6. Never go into debt to buy wants, or unnecessary things.
7. There is only one way to free yourself from the chains of debt—with saving.

Bankruptcy is the miscreant of financial freedom.

13
HOW TO SAVE ALL THE TIME

"Always bear in mind that your resolution to success
is more important than any other one thing."

Abraham Lincoln

How do you save? Maybe you could spend hundreds of dollars to buy dozens of books to learn ways to save. You will learn these tips and those tips, these examples and those examples, but you probably will not get the whole picture. You simply will not know how to *save all the time*.

You need to be saving money all the time to truly save, and make saving the key to reaching success. Most personal finance books give examples of ways to save, or devote a single chapter to savings; but they do not show you how to save *all the time*. If you come to a circumstance not presented in a book you read, you probably will not know how to save. By learning to solve problems, rather than just memorizing answers and examples, you will know how to solve any problem that presents itself.

Save Correctly—Save All the Time

To save enormous piles of money from a big percentage of your income, you need to be saving all the time. Save during more situations and your total amount of savings will be greater. Save all the time, and the savings will be the greatest.

To save 10%, generally you do not have to save most of the time; in fact, most of the time will probably be spent on *not* saving. When you save 25 to 50%, then you are saving nearly all the time. This is when saving becomes a key to reaching success. To save more, you need to use your time more wisely and devote extra time to saving. The more time spent (no pun intended!) on saving, the more money saved. In order for big savings to be possible, you need to be saving nearly all the time.

Save all the time by saving in whatever you do. Save whether you buy a necessity or something you want. Save when you earn money. Save on top of saving by saving money you earn from saving. Save when you do not buy something. Save by doing something that will produce savings. Save by using your time wisely. Save no matter what you are doing, so you are saving all the time.

When you complain about saving only a small amount, it is because you are not putting much effort into saving and are only saving in a few selected instances. Rather than saving constantly and consistently when every possibility becomes available, you are saving only once in awhile, when you feel like it. This is the cause of minute savings. "It is impossible to succeed with our money if we are intent on spending first before we save. The process of spending is a process without an ending. There is always—repeat, always—a place to spend money," wrote George M. Bowman.[1] You cannot expect enormous savings when you are putting very little effort into saving.

The Secret to Saving a Lot Is Elimination and Moderation

There are no real secrets when saving. To save enormously you need only save all the time. To save all the time you need to incorporate into your savings program the one proven method that will save you 100% all the time, each time it is used—elimination and moderation. You need to begin to live below your means—spend less than you earn—to reach your maximum savings potential. A savings program is not at full potential, and you simply are not saving correctly by saving all the time, until elimination and moderation are included.

Which is better: to save 50% on that stereo, candy bar or movie ticket, or to save 100%? When you use elimination or moderation, you save 100%.

A person does not have to eliminate wants or "things" completely to save large percentages of income. To save tremendously a person needs to eliminate to a large degree wants (thus using moderation) but becoming a miser is not necessary. This is why moderation goes together beautifully with elimination as one method. A person is moderating the total spending on wants by eliminating a majority of the spending instances. Moderation, or partial elimination, is what works the best. It saves a lot, but does not completely eliminate wants. Sure, complete elimination would save 100% all the time, every time, but that would leave you with nothing to enjoy while you save. Money should not be necessary to have fun, but who can have fun without spending at least a little money once and a while? Elimination and moderation, as one method, work so great together because they save a lot of money, but do not completely subject a person to misery and to become a miser by taking all the wants, and some fun, out of life.

Elimination and moderation make the most powerful money saving method available. Together, as one method, they can save 100% every time used. No other money-saving method can save 100% consistently!

Maximize Your Savings

To maximize your savings, you need to begin to live below your means by reducing how much you are buying. You will never reach your maximum savings potential by saving only 20% when you buy things. Rather than saving a trifle, you can save a lot by moderating your spending on wants.

Stop buying things to impress others. Stop seeking status by buying material possessions. Stop trying to keep up with the Jones' spending. Instead, start living below your means and begin maximizing your savings.

You need to work toward reaching your maximum savings potential in order for you to be saving correctly—saving all the time. For some teenagers, maximum savings potential can be as much as 80% of their take-home pay. For a single person, the maximum savings potential can be as high as 50% of take-home pay. For a family, 25% to as much as 50% may be the maximum savings potential. You need to stop saving a measly 5% and start saving correctly by reaching for your maximum savings potential!

How much can you save?
25%?
30%?
50%?
60%?

After you have created a personal savings program, you will be able to decide what your maximum savings potential is.

Too Many People Do Not Live Below Their Means

Too many people do not reach success because they are unwilling to live below their means. They are unwilling to have fewer material possessions, or wants. Sometimes people do not wish to reduce their wants. Some people believe their wants give them status, or they believe standards would be reduced if the method of elimination was introduced into their financial lives. Some people may have an addiction to a particular want, such as chocolate or video games, making it difficult to reduce how much of that want is purchased. Some people could simply have an addiction to spending—a tremendous impediment to maximizing savings through elimination and moderation. Most of the time, the reason for the absence of elimination and moderation from a savings program is that most money-saving teachers, authors and experts teach this idea of how to save money only infrequently. Whatever the reason, too many people are either ignoring or missing the greatest money saving method available.

Some people believe that their status will be lower when they buy fewer things, or wants. That may be, but imagine what all your savings will attain for your future. In order to obtain financial freedom you must be willing to sacrifice some things now in the present, to have that financial freedom in the future.

The key to remember, is that total elimination of wants is not necessary; rather, eliminate a want that should be eliminated for other reasons, including an addiction such as candy, cigarettes or excessive long-distance phone calling. Rather than worrying about how many material things are in your possession and how the method of elimination will reduce the amount, you should contemplate how using the method of elimination will make you successful through saving.

Many times, books on saving explain the method of reducing the price of a product rather than simply not buying it. To save on an expensive trip, a person is supposed to reduce the price. To save on the "fad" clothing, a person is supposed to buy on sale. To save on eating out, pop and candy, a person is supposed to use coupons, sales or some other price-reducing method. The person saves maybe 25-35% or (if the person is lucky) as much as 50%. Half savings may seem great, and there is nothing wrong with saving 50%. The problem is that the 50% is being saved on something that does not need to be purchased; thus, *100%* can be saved by not buying it! Who would rather settle for measly 50% savings when 100% is easily attainable? Moderation and elimination are *keys* to maximizing your savings potential.

Are you living *above* your means? Are you spending your way into the abyss of debt? Are the piles of bills and credit cards payments eating away all of your income and then some? Would you not rather be free from all the worry and problems that occur with debt? Would you not rather be saving your way to success? Begin now. Act immediately to begin living below your means!

Resist the Temptations

What does this mean? How do you spend less? Does this mean you have to live like a miser? No. It means you will probably increase your savings many fold. It means you will surprise yourself when you see the results. It means that you will reach success. You do it by resisting the temptation to buy the can of pop some or all of the time. Always remember that the idea is not total elimination, but using moderation and elimination together to reduce how much you buy.

Resisting the temptation to buy something every time is all it takes. A person does it by not buying the candy bar, pop, cigarettes or a beer. Stop the compact disc buying when the new ones come out, or the new clothing fad every year. Forget about what the neighbors think or that they have the fancy stuff. Eliminate the addictions of cigarettes, alcohol, gambling. Stop the compulsive spending. Stop wasting money by buying something and then throwing it out as garbage. Stop buying all those wants.

For you to have the power to resist the temptations, or any other obstacle impeding your drive to success on the road of saving, you need to invest in yourself. When you invest in yourself, you generate a personal transformation. By transforming yourself into an impregnable barrier to defeat, you are able to overcome any and all obstacles. You are able to resist any and all temptations. You are able to start your quest for success!

Back in chapter two we gave the six character traits a person must achieve in order to reach success through saving. The traits were:

- Desire
- Wholehearted work
- Discipline
- Knowledge
- Use of time and effort
- Enthusiasm

Every one of these character traits plays a role in reaching goals. Each of these traits is a part of the character of a successful person. With any of these character traits missing, the transformation from a spender to a saver will not be complete. By devoting a portion of every day's time and effort, rather than wasting time, you will achieve something every day. When you enthusiastically believe you can reach a goal, and work enthusiastically towards the goal, you will never let obstacles detour you from success. When you desire something you will do what is neccessary to acquire what you desire. By desiring something, rather than wishing for something, you move a step closer to making it become a reality. By disciplining yourself to acquire new knowledge you can use, you will be able to create plans for success that will work. Through ardent and passionate work, you will be able to accomplish what you are working on. No single trait, by itself, will procure success. You must acquire all six traits to become the best that you can be. Together, these six character traits form the great investment of yourself.

Once you have been able to resist the temptations to buy the wants, then you will be able to use elimination and moderation to maximize your savings, which in turn will allow you to reach success through saving. By investing in yourself, by believing in yourself, you will be able to do all that. By believing in yourself, by investing in yourself, you will be able to overcome all obstacles that are in your path to success.

Use Every Saving Method You Can

By itself, a single method, even if it is elimination and moderation, will not maximize your potential for saving money. The best method may be elimination and moderation, and the best way to save 100% all the time with wants or things is elimination and moderation, but the ultimate way to save the maximum possible is to use *all* the methods there are to save money. Together, as one complete savings program, all these methods will maximize your savings potential to the fullest.

To save all the time, the essence of a successful savings, you will need to save when buying need. A person cannot eliminate necessities; therefore, saving techniques other than moderation and elimination are required to be used. This is why, although elimination and moderation are great money-saving techniques, other methods need to be used to have a complete, successful personal savings program. Several excellent methods are:

- Using coupons
- Using rebates
- Comparison shopping
- Buying during sales
- Buying used

Go back to chapter three to find out more about saving when buying necessities. In that particular chapter and throughout *Saving Your Way to Success* many savings methods described will help you save money when buying necessities. In order for you to reach your savings potential by saving all the time, you need to save money when buying necessities. After reducing necessities to the actual level needed, thus taking the wants out of need, you need to reduce the money paid to buy necessities. To save all the time you need to save when buying need *and* when buying wants.

Saving all the time keeps you concentrated on your goal of reaching your maximum savings potential. To save a lot of money, you need to save all the time. To do that, savings need to be happening consistently. You need to be saving when buying needs, when buying wants and when earning. Use every savings method you can to begin saving correctly by saving all the time.

Create the Perfect Personal Savings Program

There is more to saving than saving money on what you buy or do not buy. For a complete savings program, several other saving ideas must be included:

- An expense and income record book.
- A plan to save money out of what you earn.
- An elimination of addictions.
- Education in how to do basic repairs (such as on the automobile and around the home).
- Investing your saved money wisely.

You may be able to save money without including these methods in your savings program, but to *maximize* your savings potential (thus saving correctly); you need to include these money saving methods in your savings program.

These methods are necessary components if you want to be able to save all the time. There are many things you do and decisions you make affecting your finances. If you earn a second income and if you desire to save all the time, you should automatically save a portion (or all) of that second income. If you are unwilling to have an automatic savings deduction plan to deduct a portion of your income and save every time you receive some income, then how do you expect to save all the time, which is so critically important to maximizing your savings and to reaching success through saving?

Create your own perfect personal savings program by incorporating all methods and techniques that will help you save money. If you have not already incorporated methods other than those saving you money when you buy something, you should do so immediately. Until you do, you will have only a partial savings program creating minimal results, never creating the results that are necessary for reaching success through saving. An imperfect savings program will not be very helpful in reaching success, because it does not allow you to save money all the time; therefore, you will not reach your maximum savings potential. You will reach your maximum savings potential by creating a complete savings program incorporating all types of pertinent methods for saving money.

What are some of the pertinent money saving methods and ideas you should incorporate into your savings program? The following is a summary of a few of the more important money savings methods we have discussed in *Saving Your Way to Success*.

Pay Yourself First Out of Every Paycheck

Save every time you earn money. When your paycheck comes home, save some of it. Automatically take out a sizable percentage of your hard-earned money and place it into a savings plan. If it is tough to start deducting that money, use your self-discipline (by investing in yourself), stop complaining, and start doing. If necessary, pretend the savings is an expense that has to be deducted to keep stringent accountability on constant automatic savings from every paycheck. Do what is necessary to discipline yourself to stick to your plan for reducing every paycheck automatically and placing that pre-set amount into a savings account. Do whatever is necessary to force yourself into the habit of saving money earned so success will be reachable. Whenever earnings come in, automatically save a certain percentage to ensure that you are saving."The spendthrift cannot succeed, mainly because he stands eternally in fear of poverty. Form the habit of systematic saving by putting aside a definite percentage of your income. Money in the bank gives one a very safe foundation of courage when bargaining for the sale of personal services. Without money, one must take what is offered, and be glad to get it," wrote Napoleon Hill.[2]

Set goals, strive toward them, reach them, and then set new goals. Set a goal to save $25 from each paycheck. When you reach that goal consistently, elevate the bar like a trained jumper. Raise your goal to $50. From that point, you could raise the goal to $60 or $75. You may not be able to save $75 now, but through persistence, you will be able to grow to that point. Set baby-step goals, then increase to the next level, and continue to step up with new goals until you reach success.

Keep a Record Book

This is an idea that will not actually save money in itself, but will tremendously help to save money. Keep tract of every dollar earned, spent and saved with an account book. With records, savings can become so much easier and rewarding. You will be able to watch as the savings multiply, and you will know if goals are not being reached. A record will show you your progress in striving for your maximum savings potential. Your account record book is your guide to your successful savings program. *Keeping a record book is a very powerful tool.*

Remove Addictions

An idea closely related to elimination is to stop addictions. Addictions can be in the form of anything done out of habit or obsession. They can include cigarettes, alcohol, drugs, candy, caffeine, pills, chocolate and spending. An addiction to anything is an obstacle to maximizing your savings potential. An addiction may have other consequences, but always, if it involves buying something, eats away at the pocket book like a hungry predator.

Learn How to Repair What You Own

Repair and do-it-yourself are excellent ways to save money, especially when it comes to automobile and home maintenance and repair costs. By fixing a car yourself rather than taking it to a shop, you will save as much as $45 an hour if that is what the car repair shop charges. If the repair shop charges $100 to fix something and you can do it for $50 by buying the parts and doing-it-yourself, you save $50. If you can do it in approximately an hour, you earned $45 dollars an hour rather than throwing all that money to the automobile repair shop! When you can make even small minor repairs to equipment including the lawnmower, vacuum cleaner, or even fixing a window on your home, you can save a great amount of money. Learning how to repair things you own, including your automobile, and how to do maintenance and repair around the home is a great money saving technique. Always repair and do-it-yourself rather than throwing it away or taking it to the expensive shop.

Why spend tens of thousands on a new car when a good used car for a few thousand dollars will get you where you need to go? Clearly, by buying a used automobile you will save thousands of dollars! Nearly everyone should know basic minor repair and maintenance for automobiles. It will save hundreds, if not thousands of dollars in only a few years.

Use Your Time Wisely

Stop wasting time and start using that time to save money. You can accomplish more by using time wisely rather than wasting it; thus, you can save more. Rather than wasting time by watching television, clip coupons and go through grocery store advertisements while watching television to use the time more wisely. Better yet, reduce how much television you watch and use that time more wisely to save more money and reach success.

Time, because it can not be regained, should and must be used wisely all of the time. Use time more purposefully to clean out the garage, to fix that broken leg on the coffee table or to work toward reaching your goals. Rather than complain there is not enough time, cut out things that are wasting time, such as television, and then use your time for the things for which you normally say, "I do not have the time." You cannot bring time back. You cannot save time. Time is so precious that it is the most precious commodity there is. Once used for something, it becomes the past, and whatever became of the use of that time is here to stay.

No one controls time; yet, everyone has the same amount of time. The people who reach success on their own are the people who use their time wisely. They know time is precious, yet they have the same amount of time as everyone else. Everyone is equal. The billion-dollar man has no advantage over the million-dollar man, nor does the million-dollar man have an advantage over the hundred-dollar man. Everyone on earth is equal because time, the most valuable commodity on earth, is free to all. What matters is how the time is used. Use it wisely and great things can happen. Use time poorly and laziness will happen. Do not think the millionaires have an advantage over a person who is poor. They all have the same twenty-four hours in the day—the same twenty-four hours in the day you have and use. It only matters how you use it.

Invest Wisely

"By saving $200 a month from the age of 20 to the age of 65 and putting it away into solid mutual funds invested in the American stock market, you will be a millionaire when you retire," wrote Brian Tracy.[3] Saving is the key to reaching financial freedom, but if you desire for your money to grow, you need to invest it wisely.

Keys to investing wisely are time perspective and self-discipline. Rather than investing foolishly on the market's short term ups and downs, you need to have the self-discipline to invest for the long term. Sacrifice is the key for long term wealth accumulation. The willingness to sacrifice a few things now in order to enjoy wealth and success in the future is the key to your financial prosperity.

Work Hard, Save Hard

If you have maximized your savings, but you have the desire to save more, you need only earn more. A secondary income is a great ingredient for a savings program. If you are able to earn more through hard work and persistence, you will be able to save more. If you are able to save more, you will be able to move faster toward success through saving. Use your abilities and intuition to develop a plan creating a secondary income.

You can only move forward in your drive for financial freedom by saving more or earning more. By saving more *and* earning more, you will move forward doubly as fast. By acquiring a second income, whether it is a part-time job or a side-line business, you will have more money to save—moving you forward in your drive for success and financial freedom.

Wholehearted work is also a part of investing in yourself. When you work hard, you will be able to reach goals. When you work hard, you will be able to earn more. Hard work is a key to more money saved.

Use the Four R's of Recycling

The four R's of recycling help save the environment, but they also can do something else: save money. Many people who save, although they may adamantly oppose recycling, may actually be doing at least one of the four R's. The same is true for people who do use the four R's for helping the environment. They do not often think of it as saving money, but it is. The four R's do help save the environment, but they are also an excellent method to saving a lot of money.

Reduce how much garbage you throw out. Reuse things. Repair broken or worn down products. Recycle your recyclables. All of these can save money. By reducing how much is thrown out, you can save money, because it means less money that was paid for the products is being thrown out as garbage. Stop throwing out your money as "garbage"!

Reuse things to multiply their worth and reduce your garbage. Using a product twice, when it was intended to have only one use, doubles its value. If a dollar was paid for the one-use product, and two uses came out of it, then each cost only 50 cents rather than $1. This equals a 100% increase in value and 100% savings on the other instance of buying the eliminated product.

Repairing the couch, car and lawnmower will save money by not taking them to expensive repair shops, by reducing garbage and by increasing the products' value. When recycling, you can earn money—but more importantly you reduce the amount of money being thrown out as garbage. By recycling, you are also earning money when you bring the recyclables to the recycling center. All four of the R's that help the environment can and do help the pocketbook.

Use the Power of Self-Discipline

After reading about all of these money saving methods and techniques, you may believe there is no more—but there is. There is still a missing ingredient, one that cannot be left out of a savings program. This ingredient is ten times more powerful than the method of elimination or any other savings idea or method. This ingredient will, on its own, make or break your plan of using saving to reaching success. This ingredient is *you*.

Finally, but most importantly, you must start thinking "save," rather than "spend" and you must start doing it. That is how *you* will become a success through saving. When you invest in yourself and actually discipline yourself to start saving money, you will be able to maximize your savings potential and you will then be able to reach success through saving. Only when you begin to habituate yourself through self-discipline to constantly think "save" rather than "spend," to change yourself into a saver, will you be able to accumulate wealth.

The most basic, necessary element of saving is the will power to do it. If there is no will power to eliminate wants, stop addictions, use an account book, stop spending and start saving, then it simply will not happen. The more will power to save, the more saved. If you do little, you will save little. The amount of effort going into saving directs how much will be received from your efforts.

You—your will power and your courage, strength, abilities, talents, goals, dreams, experience and knowledge—are the last ingredient, the last opportunity, the key to becoming successful. No one can do it for you. No method, idea or concept will do it for you. No book or knowledge will do it for you. Saving will not do it for you. Nothing will make you a success unless you desire it passionately to and then use it. *You* are the key to your success.

By following the proven methods and techniques discussed throughout *Saving Your Way to Success*, anyone can become successful. You are one of those people who can become successful through saving. You may not become super rich, but you will become financially free. Rather than being frustrated all the time over your finances, you will have peace of mind. Instead of being chained to debt and having your life controlled by those chains and the people that operate them, by saving your way to success, you will become independent and self-reliant. No longer will you feel disconsolate; the emotion of happiness will radiate throughout you once you have reached success. Saving has the power to change you into a self-reliant, happy, independent success.

Use your own talents, abilities and self-mastery to be able to invest in yourself and move yourself toward success on the road of saving. It may be the road less traveled, but that is what makes success so much sweeter. Stop taking the road everyone else is taking. Stop being a follower and become a leader. Take the initiative and move outside the monotony of the crowd. Become the navigator of your own success by taking the road of savings, rather than continuing to allow spending to dictate your life. When an obstacle appears along the road, do not abandon your goals; use your own inventiveness, ambition and motivation to conquer the obstacles trying to thwart your drive for success. *Take the initiative and begin utilizing saving to reach your success!*

Points to Ponder:

- The key to saving enormous amounts of money and using that savings to reach success is to save correctly by saving all the time.
- A person cannot expect enormous savings when the person is putting very little effort into saving.
- By reducing how much wants you buy through self-discipline, you will be taking a giant step forward towards maximizing your savings potential.
- To fully maximize your savings potential, you need to save all the time by using every money saving technique, method, and idea that you can.
- Create the perfect personal savings program by taking the following steps:

1. Create a plan of automatic savings deductions from all income.
2. Create an income and expense record book.
3. Eliminate all addictions.
4. Learning small household repair and simple do-it-yourself automobile maintenance and repair.
5. Begin budgeting your time to use it wisely.
6. Acquire a second income through ardent and passionate work.
7. Using recycling to reduce, reuse, and repair, rather than throwing away your money as garbage.
8. Most importantly, to fully maximize your savings potential, in order to reach success, you must constantly think "save." Through the power of self-discipline, you will be able to reach success through saving.

Only when you begin to habituate yourself through self-discipline to constantly think "save" rather than "spend" to change yourself into a saver, will you be able to accumulate wealth.

Footnotes:

Chapter 1:

1. *Home Book of Quotations*, Dodd, Mead and Company, Inc. 1958.
2. Napoleon Hill, *Think and Grow Rich*, Hawthorn Book, Inc., 1937.
3. Adam Smith, *An Inquiry Into the Nature and Causes of the Wealth of Nations*, Random House, Inc., 1965.
4. "Life in 2018," Banc One Investment Advisors Corporation, 1998.
5. Walter Updegrave, "Hey, Big Spender: Is Our Low National Savings Rate a Real Problem or a False Alarm?" *Money,* April 1, 2002 v31 i4 p. 59.
6. George M. Bowman, *How to Succeed with Your Money*, The Moody Bible Institute of Chicago, 1974.
7. Michael Jackman, *Business & Economic Quotations*, Macmillian Publishing Company, 1984.
8. *Home Book of Quotations,* Dodd, Mead and Company, Inc., 1958.
9. Adam Smith, *An Inquiry Into the Nature and Causes of the Wealth of Nations*, Random House, Inc., 1965.
10. *Home Book of Quotations,* Dodd, Mead and Company, Inc., 1958.
11. *Home Book of Quotations*, Dodd, Mead and Company, Inc., 1958.
12. Henry David Thoreau, *Walden*, chapter 18, 1854.

Chapter 2:

1. Napoleon Hill, *Think and Grow Rich*, Hawthorn Book, Inc., 1937.
2. Burton Stevenson, *The Economist*, Volume 343, June 7, 1997, page 25.
3. Burton Stevenson, *The Economist*, Volume 343, June 7, 1997, page 25.

4. "Life in 2018," Banc One Investment Advisors Corporation, 1998.
5. Walter Updegrave, "Hey, Big Spender: Is Our Low National Savings Rate a real Problem or a False Alram?" *Money*, April 1, 2002 v31 i4 p.59.
6. Napoleon Hill, *Think and Grow Rich*, Hawthorn Book, Inc., 1937.
7. *Home Book of Quotations,* Dodd, Mead and Company, Inc., 1958.
8. Norman Vincent Peale, *Enthusiasm Makes the Difference*, Fawcett World Library, 1967.

Chapter 3:

1. *Home Book of Quotations,* Dodd, Mead and Company, Inc., 1958.
2. Seneca *Epistulae ad Lucilium*, Epis. XXXI, 3.
3. Kate MacArthur, "Overstuffed; Americans are Eating Out Less as the Economy Falters." *Advertising Age,* August 13, 2001 v72 p. 3.
4. Ibid.
5. *Money*, December, 1995.
6. Glen Bland, *Success! the Glen Bland Method*, Tyndale House Publishers, Inc. 1977.

Chapter 4:

1. *Home Book of Quotations,* Dodd, Mead and Company, Inc., 1958.
2. *Home Book of Quotations,* Dodd, Mead and Company, Inc., 1958.
3. Vance Packard, *Status Seekers*, David McKay Co., Inc., April, 1959.

Chapter 5:

1. *Home Book of Quotations,* Dodd, Mead and Company, Inc., 1958.
2. Ibid.
3. Benjamin Franklin, *Poor Richard's Almanac*, 1758
4. Michael Jackman, *Business & Economic Quotations,* Macmillian Publishing Company, 1984.
5. Robert G. Allen, *Creating Wealth.* Simon and Schuster, Inc., 1983.
6. Janet Bodnar, *Kiplinger's Money Smart Kids*, The Kiplinger Washington Editors, Inc., 1993.
7. Kathy M. Kristof, "Consumer Bankruptices Climb by 15.1%." *Los Angeles Times*, May 17, 2002 p.C-3
8. Adam Smith, *An Inquiry Into the Nature and Causes of the Wealth of Nations*, Random House, Inc., 1965.
9. Janet Bodnar, *Kiplinger's Money Smart Kids*, The Kiplinger Washington Editors, Inc., 1993.
10. Ibid.
11. Ibid.

Chapter 6:

1. *Home Book of Quotations,* Dodd, Mead and Company, Inc., 1958.
2. Meghan Carleton, "Teen Spending Continues to Grow with Teen Population." *Tribune Business News*, June 30, 2002.
3. Adam Smith, *An Inquiry Into the Nature and Causes of the Wealth of Nations*, Random House, Inc., 1965.
4. Michael Jackman, *Business & Economic Quotations.* Macmillian Publishing Company., 1984.
5. Ibid.
6. Joyce M. Rosenberg, "Young People Save Saving for the future," *The Forum*, October 9, 1999. AP.
7. Janet Bodnar, *Kiplinger's Money Smart Kids*, The Kiplinger Washington Editors, Inc., 1993.
8. Joyce M. Rosenberg, "Young People Save Saving for the future," *The Forum*, October 9, 1999. AP.

Chapter 7:

1. *Home Book of Quotations,* Dodd, Mead and Company, Inc., 1958.
2. Ibid.
3. Robert G. Allen, *Creating Wealth,* Simon and Schuster, Inc., 1983.
4. Napoleon Hill, *Think and Grow Rich*, Hawthorn Book, Inc., 1937.
5. Michael Jackman, *Business & Economic Quotations*, Macmillian Publishing Company, 1984.

Chapter 8:

1. *Home Book of Quotations,* Dodd, Mead and Company, Inc., 1958.
2. Ibid.
3. *Business Week*, September 5, 1994, page 36.
4. Deborah Rankin, "Start Now- Retire Early." *Reader's Digest*, February 1998, page 98-101.
5. *Home Book of Quotations.* Dodd, Mead and Company, Inc., 1958.
6. Roger Lowenstein, "An Unassuming billionaire." *Reader's Digest*, March 1996, page 87-91.

Chapter 9:

1. *Home Book of Quotation*, Dodd, Mead and Company, Inc., 1958.
2. *Webster's New Twentieth Century Dictionary*, William Collinst World Publishing Co., Inc., 1975.
3. Diane MacEachern, *Save Our Planet*, Dell Publishing Group, Inc., 1990.
4. *Webster's New Twentieth Century Dictionary*, William Collinst World Publishing Co., Inc., 1975.
5. Nancy Allen, "Composting Food Scarps at Georgia Prison," *BioCycle,* April, 1994, page 90.

6. *Science World*, December 9, 1994, volume 51, page 6-18.
7. Vance Packard, *The Waste Makers*, Pocket Books, 1969.
8. *EPA Journal*, Volume 25, Winter 1995, page 18-19.

Chapter 10

1. *Home Book of Quotations,* Dodd, Mead and Company, Inc., 1958.
2. 10 Kelly Baron, "Each Week We Waste..." *Forbes*, October 16, 2000 p. 158.
3. *American Demographic*, March 1993, Volume 15, Page 50-54.
4. *Home Book of Quotations,* Dodd, Mead and Company, Inc., 1958.
5. George M. Bowman*, How to Succeed with Your Money*, The Moody Bible Institute of Chicago, 1974.
6. *Better Homes and Gardens*, Volume 74, February 1996, page 48-49.
7. "Cartoon Causes Illness in Japanese Children." AP. *The Forum*, December 17, 1997.
8. *Home Book of Quotations,* Dodd, Mead and Company, Inc., 1958.

Chapter 11:

1. Michael Jackman, *Business & Economic Quotations,* Macmillian Publishing Company, 1984.
2. Scott Burns, "It's really very simple: Just spend less than you earn." *The Forum*, AP. February 10, 1991.

Chapter 12:

1. *Home Book of Quotations,* Dodd, Mead and Company, Inc., 1958.
2. Kathy M. Kristof, "Consumer Bankruptcies Climb by 15.1%." *Los Angeles Times*, May 17, 2002 p. C-3.
3. Burton Stevenson, *The Economist*, Volume 343, June 7, 1997, page 25.

4. John M. Barron; Gregory Elliehausen; Michael E. Staten "Monitoring the Household Sector with Aggregate Credit Bureau Data," *Business Economics*, January 2000 v35 i1 P63.
5. Terry Savage, "The Savage Truth on Money," PBS March 11, 2000.
6. Jacqueline M. Graves, "Credit Cards, a Buyer's Market," *Fortune*, June 27, 1994, page 13-6.
7. "The Perils of Plastic," *Business Week*, Feb 14, 2000 i3668 p127.
8. Terry Savage, "The Savage Truth on Money," PBS March 11, 2000.
9. Ann Landers, "Daughter's Credit debt Worries Mom." AP, *The Forum*, December 31, 1998.
10. *Home Book of Quotations,* Dodd, Mead and Company, Inc., 1958.

Chapter 13:

1. George M. Bowman, *How to Succeed with Your Money*, The Moody Bible Institute of Chicago, 1974.
2. Napoleon Hill, *Think and Grow Rich*, Hawthorn Book, Inc., 1937.
3. Brian Tracy, *The Luck Factor*, Nightingale-Conant Coporation, 1997.

Dear Reader,

I wrote this book espically for you. I want you to succeed with the money you earn. Because you bought this book says a lot in itself. However, I caution you by saying merely reading my book will not bring you success with your money. You must apply the principles of *Saving Your Way to Success* to your life. Study these principles; think about them until they become a part of your subconscious mind.

Moreover, don't expect riches to come to you overnight. My money-saving system will teach you how to build wealth over time. As you become more skillful in applying these principles, the faster you will be able to build your wealth and attain peace of mind.

Let me hear from you as you have fun *saving your way to success*. I would like to share your success story with others. Please write me at the following address:

Justin P. Ertelt
P.O. Box 86
Fargo, ND 58107

Sincerely Yours,

Justin P. Ertelt

About The Author

Justin P. Ertelt has learned from years of personal experience, observation, research, and study that saving is the key to personal financial success. Far from a dry academic study, his book is filled with Justin's real-life experiences and keen observations—qualities that make this book a dynamic and useful tool.

With bankruptcies at an all-time high—while savings have reached an all-time low—Justin felt compelled to develop a savings program for everyday working people who are trying to balance a debt with a serious lack of savings. Justin's mission in *Saving Your Way to Success* is to deliver an important message—saving is the key to success—and show readers how to use it to enrich their lives and reach financial independence.

Justin lives in Fargo, North Dakota. He has won numerous awards in areas of interest including writing and newsletter publishing. He is currently saving his own way to success.

Printed in the United States
58710LVS00001B/31